THE THIRD TOUR
OF
DOCTOR SYNTAX
IN SEARCH OF A WIFE
A POEM

WITH TWENTY-FIVE
COLOURED ILLUSTRATIONS
BY THOMAS ROWLANDSON

A NEW EDITION

NEW YORK
D. APPLETON & COMPANY
1903

NOTE

THIS Issue is founded on the Edition published by R. Ackermann in the year 1821

PREFACE

THIS prolonged work, is, at length, brought to a close.—It has grown to this size, under rare and continuing marks of public favour; while the same mode of Composition has been employed in the last, as in the former Volumes.——They are all equally indebted to Mr. Rowlandson's talents.

It may, perhaps, be considered as presumptuous in me, and at my age, to sport even with my own Dowdy Muse, but, from the extensive patronage which Doctor Syntax has received, it may be presumed that, more or less, he has continued to amuse: And I, surely, have no reason to be dissatisfied, when Time points at my eightieth Year, that I can still afford some pleasure to those who are disposed to be pleased.

The AUTHOR.

Directions for placing the Plates

Dr. Syntax setting out in search of a Wife	*Frontispiece*	
Illustrated Title Page		
Soliloquising	*To face p.*	10
Turn'd Nurse	,,	31
The Banns forbidden	,,	83
With a Blue Stocking Beauty	,,	90
The Cellar Quartetto	,,	120
Presenting a Floral Offering	,,	129
The Billiard Table	,,	132
Misfortune at Tulip Hall	,,	134
The Harvest Home	,,	138
The Garden Trio	,,	151
At a Card Party	,,	154
Star-Gazing	,,	157
In the wrong Lodging House	,,	182
Received by the Maid instead of the Mistress	,,	194
The Artist's Room	,,	198
Death of Punch	,,	202
The Advertisement for a Wife	,,	210
The Foundling	,,	213
The Result of purchasing a blind Horse	,,	221
A Noble Hunting Party	,,	242
Introduction to Courtship	,,	250
In Danger	,,	262
Funeral of Dr. Syntax	,,	264

A TOUR
IN
SEARCH OF A WIFE

CANTO XXXIV

HOW is it none contented lives
  With the fair lot which reason gives,
Or chance presents or labour gains!
Why in our pleasures or our pains
Does want disturb or envy wound,
And calm enjoyment's rarely found?
—May not this answer meet the ear,
That life is not th' appointed sphere,
Where, by the wise design of Heaven,
A cloudless joy is ever given?
For that e'en virtue's self must wait
Till death has clos'd our mortal state;
And then our virtue's promis'd meed
Of endless pleasure will succeed.

'Tis true experience sage has said,
And as a real truth pourtray'd,
That happy hours may be our own,
But happy days are never known.

The morn may smile, the noon may weep,
While pain at night may banish sleep:
Our own or some dear friend's distress
May check a smiling happiness;
E'en while it mantles on the brow
The heart may feel a sense of woe.
Thus throughout life 'tis man's frail nature
To be a discontented creature.
Indeed, we must the truth confess,
How oft we look for happiness
From what we never may possess;
But ask, in life's continu'd chase,
For change of things and change of place,
And as our real good pursue,
What we behold in distant view,
Beyond possession's present hour;—
'Tis that we wish within our power,
And o'er a something seem to brood,
Contrasted with our present good.

   If you ask where doth dwell content
'Neath cot or lofty battlement,
Whether in car of state it ride
Or by the humble peasant's side;
Or in the court of kings doth dwell
Or in the hermit's lonely cell?
Say does it dance in lover's bower,
Or pass in smiles the rural hour?
Do laurel wreaths entwine it round,
Or is it at the banquet found?
Say does it crouch 'neath Cupid's wing,
Or play upon the minstrel's string?
No—this is the keen mind's reply,
Such is the world's philosophy.
—When in the car of state you ride
Content is by the peasant's side:

Whene'er you gaze from mountain's brow
You see him in the vale below;
And when you join the courtly train,
He doth appear a rustic swain.
Nay, when in splendid halls you're seen,
He dances on the village green.
Thus in vain your time is spent,
For never will you find content.
As you pursue, he flies for ever,
Ne'er will you overtake him—never.
Or high or low, whate'er our lot,
We view him on some envied spot,
But dimly seen, where we are not.

Broken with toils, with arms opprest,
The soldier thinks the merchant blest,
Who calmly sits at home at ease,
While fortune, with her fav'ring breeze,
Wafts him her treasures o'er the seas.
And when the threat'ning tempests rise,
War is my choice the merchant cries;
For battle ends th' hero's story,
Or brings him death or gives him glory.
—When the country 'Squire is seen
At number six in Lincoln's-Inn,
With healthy look and ruddy face
To give his fee and state his case,
The wearied lawyer 'midst his books,
With gaping yawn and pallid looks,
Longs to buy lands and country-seat
To give him health and calm retreat;
While as th' admiring client's eye
Beholds the vast variety
Of stately forms and the gay measure
Of each embroider'd scene of pleasure

Which the vast city's limits give,
He longs in Portland-Place to live.[1]

As we pass life's uncertain day,
We may submit, but must obey;
And all that we are call'd to do,
Is to keep virtue in our view,
Not all the dignity of power
Can quicken life's sad, lagging hour;
Nor glutted avarice impart
A pleasure to the aching heart.
If fortune's gifts you truly rate,
Then tell me what would mend your state.
If real joy on wealth is built,
Villains might comfort find in guilt:
But when he sees th' encreasing store
The Miser's fears encrease the more.
Is happiness the point in view?
I mean the real and the true;
She nor in camps nor courts resides,
Nor in the humble cottage bides:
Seek her alike in ev'ry sphere,
Where virtue is, for she is there.
'Tis to no rank of life confin'd,
But dwells in ev'ry honest mind,
As much, at least, as e'er is known
For mortal man to call his own.

---

[1] O fortunati mercatores! gravis armis
Miles ait, multo jam fractus membra labore.
Contra Mercator, navim jactantibus Austris,
Militia est potior. Quid enim? concurritor: horæ
Momento cita mors venit, aut victoria læta.
Agricolam laudat juris legumque peritus,
Sub galli cantum consultor ubi ostia pulsat.
Ille, datis vadibus, qui rure extractus in urbem est,
Solos felices viventes clamat in urbe.
      Hor. Sat. Lib. i.

To shine and glitter all in gold,
To be in words and science bold,
Wealth to enjoy and dainty fare,
The monarch's friend, the people's care;
To all that's gay and proud and great,
Although such gifts may elevate,
The groaning gout, and racking stone
May change the mirth to bitter moan.
But e'en though sickness ne'er annoys,
Riches and honours are but toys,
If Conscience be not firm and free,
And wrapp'd in its fidelity.
The peaceful conscience is the boon
That keeps the jarring mind in tune:
O 'tis the heart's so cheering guest,
Which had—a rush for all the rest.

Thus Syntax, as he view'd the throng
Who sped the jovial hours along,
And took a short-liv'd leave of care,
Amid the gambols of a fair,
From Rect'ry porch indulg'd the hour
In letting loose his well-known power,
When, without any social friend,
He did his studious mind unbend.
Thus with many a maxim fraught
That play'd upon his busy thought,
He from his easy-chair arose
And did again his thoughts disclose
That bore the air, though 'twas not meant,
Of calm but tender discontent.

"The WORTHIES now have left their home
For many a week or month to come;
And since their heiress has been tied
In wedlock and become a bride,

They with parental joy imprest
Are now their daughter's welcome guest.
Thus since my much-lov'd friends are gone,
I feel what 'tis to be alone.
Nor do my Classic shelves supply
The cheerless dull vacuity:
They help to pass an hour away,
But cannot serve me through the day;
While sluggard time appears to crawl
Through the unwelcome interval:
Nor does my reason feel it good
To lead this life of solitude.
With many a blessing I must own,
I'm almost discontented grown,
And if I check it not ere long
I shall be thinking very wrong:
Some foreign help-mates I must call
To aid me ere this sense inthrall
My spirits, 'gainst whose powers I preach
And prove the doctrines which I teach.
—Besides when I am thus alone
I think upon my Dolly gone:
I see her wheresoe'er I stray
In open walk or woodland way.
When I an ev'ning saunter take
Beside the margin of the lake,
I recollect the tender charm
When she hung fondly on my arm,
Where, when the day was almost done,
We had talk'd down the ev'ning sun.
Nay I perceive my erring mind
Is to her loss far less resign'd,
Than when the power we must obey,
Consign'd her to her native clay;
Nay, resignation, ev'ry hour
Appears to lose its wholesome power.

IN SEARCH OF A WIFE

This is not as it ought to be,
Nor reason, nor philosophy,
Nor pious duty can forbear
To disapprove such worldly care.
If then this lonely life appears
T' engender sighs and ask for tears,
I must th' untoward system change,
In wider fields of converse range;
Nor fear to mingle in the strife,
As chance directs, that chequers life;
And, by new, varying, scenes restore
My mind to what it was before.
Though my earlier years have been
Of study the laborious scene,
Yet social pleasure bore a part
To quicken sense and cheer the heart;
Nor did my spirits ever feel
When at the foot of fortune's wheel,
And life scarce knew its due supply,
The tremors of despondency;
Such as of late I'm doom'd to find
The jaundic'd temper of the mind.
What's to be done, how can I cure
This restless something I endure?
A learn'd Divine, it may be said,
Should know where to apply for aid,
And he who doth to others preach,
Should have the means himself to teach.
It is not that my mind's embued
With any act of turpitude;
'Tis not an error deep and grave,
That doth the virtuous wish enslave,
Which may awake the fear of Heaven,
And doubts it may not be forgiven;
That doth for pale repentance call
To change the sorrowing prodigal;

No, 'tis the feeling heart's vagary
Which chance may give and time may vary:
That from some nat'ral cause arises,
Which neither angers, nor surprises:
But still it plagues while it doth last,
Nor must we let it hold us fast;
For should we not its power oppose
At length it into habit grows,
And may become a rooted feature
T' encrease the weaknesses of nature;
While full enough, none will contest,
Are to be found among the best.
But is he not the weakest, who
Suffers his fancy to pursue
That train of thought which may augment
The source of idle discontent?
And after all, 'tis this same folly
That serves to make me melancholy.
'Tis plain then, I have nought to do,
But these weak symptoms to subdue,
From this dull slumb'ring to awake,
From these disheart'ning thoughts to break,
To form new schemes, to leave off talking,
And set my better mind a walking."

Here Syntax paus'd and silent stood,
In grave and contemplative mood,
When ancient Madge, who wound the reel,
And gave the movement to her wheel,
Tow'rds Heaven appear'd to cast her eye
And gave a deep and heart-felt sigh.

Old Marg'ret, of a village race,
Was the sage gran'nam of the place.
The dame had pass'd her early day
In service of the great and gay;

And was well pleas'd to have it known,
What stations she had held in town;
Would gravely boast where she had been,
And tell the fine things she had seen:
In short, at threescore years of age,
She was become a rural sage.
It is not needful to relate
What was her lot in married state;
'Twas like what others feel, who try
Their chance in marriage lott'ry.
But time had pass'd full many a year,
Since she first shed a widow's tear,
And now she rul'd in due degree,
The household of the Rectory;
Where she did all her duties tend,
Less as a servant than a friend.

   And now old Margaret sigh'd again
As if she suffer'd real pain;
When Syntax thus the dame address'd—
"What anxious thought disturbs your breast,
And wherefore do you lift your eye
As if commercing with the sky?"
Now Madge it seems had caught the sense
Of all the Doctor's eloquence,
And, with kind feelings for her guide,
She thus, in measur'd speech, replied—
"It is not for myself I sue
To Heaven's mercy, 'tis for you.
I could well scold you if I dare,
And your whims almost make me swear;
You may keep talking on for ever
'Twill never do you good, no never.
What is your fending and your proving,
'Tis nonsense all—I say, keep moving.

Do you not hear what pleasures reign
Among the croud on yonder plain?
Quit, my sad Sir, that odious chair,
With your grave melancholy air,
And join the pastimes of the fair.
See 'midst the bustle what is done,
Look on the sports and view the fun:
Who knows but a good donkey race
May plant a smile upon your face.
Of this I'm sure, that when you see
The scene of harmless revelry,
And from the happy people hear
The untaught joke, the merry jeer,
Their honest pleasures will impart
Smiles to your sympathising heart.
You know the joy your flock will share
To view their much-lov'd pastor there;—
And when you see how they receive it,
You'll feel it two-fold, you who give it.
Do as I say—you'll find it right,
'Twill prove a most enliv'ning sight,
And save you from a restless night.
Keep moving—quit your studious labours,
Set off and visit all your neighbours.
A change of scene, a change of place,
Will from your mind these whimsies chase,
And soon I with delight shall see
My master from his meagrims free."

Syntax.

"Thank you for that, my vet'ran lady,
I'll go and try to get a gay day;
'Twas rare, sound common-sense, that brought
Such good advice into your thought.
To-morrow, I'll clap spurs to horse,
And, in good earnest, take my course

Drawn by Rowlandson

IN SEARCH OF A WIFE

To *Billy Bumpkin,* who will greet me
With his loud laughs, and kindly treat me:
Yes, with his broad-face mirth he'll try
The power of hospitality."

On the next morn his breakfast done,
With not a cloud to hide the sun,
The Doctor did his way pursue,
And, in a trotting hour or two
Bumpkin's old hall appear'd in view.
When soon he saw its hearty host
Leaning most idly 'gainst a post,
And letting loose loud fits of laughter
To see boys bathing in the water;
Who with their splash of mud and mire
Amus'd the humour of the 'Squire.

Syntax, in sober, solemn state,
With Pat behind drew near the gate;
And when he their approach espied,
Bill Bumpkin clapp'd his hands and cried;
"My worthy Parson is it you?
The same i' fackins, I've in view.
Six months, I think, are gone and past
And more since I beheld you last!
Whate'er I knew I left at college,
And you like none but men of knowledge;
Yet, in plain English, I declare,
I do delight to see you here.
I have no learn'd or Latin lingo,
But a fresh tap of foaming stingo,
Which will make you to jabber Greek,
As nat'rally as pigs can squeak.
And, if your heart is out of tune,
Will make you long to stride the moon."

"—Not quite so high as that my friend,
But something which doth that way tend:
Not quite so high," the Doctor said,
"But yet some choice enliv'ning aid
My slacken'd spirits have in view
When I pay my respects to you;
For here, I'm sure, that humour gay
And the frank smile will crown the day.
You, my good-hearted friend, must know
The cause of my domestic woe.
Of my friends too I am bereft,
The WORTHIES have the country left,
And when they may return to cheer
My drooping heart doth not appear:—
Thus dulness now is found to reign
Within the verge of *Sommerden*,
And doth a full possession take
Of its fair borders of the Lake.
Thus 'tis my joyless fate to roam
For comfort that's not found at home."
"—Then find it here," replied the 'Squire,
"New scenes will other thoughts inspire,
My means of pleasure you shall share:
I'll teach you how to banish care."

Though Syntax did not trust the skill
That such a promise would fulfil,
He gave assent with nodding head,
And follow'd where his leader led.
He took the Doctor through his grounds,
Display'd his kennel and his hounds,
Their diff'rent ages, old and young,
Their speed, their noses and their tongue;
Then order'd forth his hunting stud,
Dwelt on their merits and their blood;

While to their diff'rent feats, and more,
The green-clad huntsman stoutly swore.
He then described some arduous chase
That did his Nimrod annals grace;
Show'd many a brush that cover'd o'er
The purlieus of the kennel door:
Nor did a hero ever prize
The trophies gain'd in victories
Whose flutt'ring ensigns might display
The pride of many a well-fought day,
With more exulting sense of fame,
Than *Bumpkin* told the boasted name,
Which his equestrian powers command
Among the woods of Westmoreland.

The Doctor heard and made pretence
To listen to his eloquence;
But though with certain science fraught,
It could not charm his serious thought;
Nor did it seem to chase away
The gloomy humour of the day.

"Why still so grave my worthy friend,"
The 'Squire exclaim'd, "where will this end?
I prithee, why make all this pother;
You've lost one wife—then get another;
And sure, in all this country round,
Another may be quickly found.
From different motives people grieve,
For wives that die and wives that live.
—That scare-crow Death is oft a sad one,
Takes the good wife and leaves the bad one,
As sure as that bright sun doth shine,
I wish that he had taken mine.
Not that I suffer such disaster
As to let madam play the master,

Nor yet, to let the lady boast
That o'er her lord she rules the roast.
I learn'd not, where I went to school,
In such a way to play the fool.
'Tis true from harshness I refrain,
But then I always hold the rein:
For he who ventures on a wife,
To be the comfort of his life,
Should never this advice refuse:—
Take her down in her wedding shoes."
—Syntax his fancy to beguile
Here sunk his laughter in a smile.
For it was known to great and small
How things went on at Bumpkin-Hall:
Nay, 'twas a well-known standing joke,
Among the neighb'ring country folk,
That when the lady's in the way
The 'Squire would ne'er say yea or nay
But as her ruling spirit told him,
Or with a certain look control'd him:
Though now his tongue ne'er seem'd to rest,
And thus his invitation press'd.—
" Doctor come here, next hunting-season,
And faith, my friend, I'll show you reason;
You shall mount on my Yorkshire grey,
And gallop all your cares away."
" I doubt not," Syntax smiling said,
" Your recipe would be obey'd;
It would afford a speedy cure
For every evil I endure;
But for my kind physician's sake,
I do not wish my neck to break."

They talk'd, when soon the bell's shrill chime
Declar'd it to be dinner time,

Nor was it an unwelcome call
That bade their footsteps seek the hall;
For though the Doctor's whims prevail'd,
His appetite had never fail'd.
By madam he was kindly greeted,
As, "How d'ye do?" and "pray be seated.
It doth a perfect age appear
Since we enjoy'd your presence here;
I feel it always as a treasure,
And wish I oft'ner felt the pleasure."
"*Bumpkin, I pray you move the dish,
And help the Doctor to some fish.*"
"Indeed I hope, 'tis in your view
To pass with us a day or two.
Nay I could wish it might be more,
And lengthen'd out into a score."
"*Bumpkin, you think not as we dine,
That some folks love a glass of wine.*"
"I have not seen you for an hour,
Since you have made your charming Tour,
And I shall ask you to display
Its hist'ry in your rapid way."
"*Husband, I'll bet my life upon it,
Our kind guest's plate has nothing on it;
Make haste and give it a supply
Of that well-looking pigeon-pye.*"
"'Tis a fine match Miss Worthy made:
A charming girl, I always said;
And does those qualities possess
That claim the promis'd happiness.
Some may think one thing, some another;
But is she handsome as her mother?
Her mamma's auburn locks, I own,
Are better than her daughter's brown,
Although the latter you may see,
Dame nature has bestow'd on me."

"*'Squire Bumpkin, were it not my care
To see how all about me fare,
Our Rev'rend friend would have good luck,
To get a wing of that fine duck.*"
" Since, Doctor, you were here before,
I've added to my Floral store,
And some fine specimens have got
Which are not ev'ry Florist's lot,
They're in the happiest state to view,
And will be much admir'd by you."
"*As some folk do not seem to think,
That when we eat, we want to drink,
I ask you, Doctor, if you'll join
Your Hostess in a glass of W*INE*?
Your better taste, Sir, will prevail,
Nor share in vulgar cups of A*LE*.*"
" My new Piano has a tone
Which your judicious ear will own,
At least to me it so appears,
Such as one very seldom hears.
I too of late have practis'd much,
And am improv'd in time and touch;
Thus with your fiddle's well-known power,
We shall delight an evening hour."

 The Doctor made his frequent bow,
And *yes* replied, or answer'd *no*,
Just as the lady's words requir'd,
Or as his empty plate inspir'd.
Indeed, it clearly must appear
He'd nought to do but eat and hear;
While the calm Husband's sharpen'd knife
Obey'd the orders of his Wife.

 Thus Madam, with habitual art,
Continued her presiding part;

Did with her smiles the Doctor crown,
Or silence Billy with a frown;
And, in a well-adapted measure,
Alternately display'd her pleasure;
Her tongue was never at a stand,
But play'd at Question and Command:
She could affirm and could deny
With mild impetuosity,
And scarce her question could be heard,
Ere she an answer had preferr'd:
Thus, till the absence of the cloth,
She to and fro employ'd them both;
At once th' attention to delight
And give a grace to appetite.

The dinner pass'd as dinners do;
Ma'am's health was drunk and she withdrew;
But as the lady left the chair
With solemn smile but gracious air,
"Doctor," she said, "I know your taste
Is not your time and thoughts to waste
In that intemp'rance which gives birth
To boist'rous noise and vulgar mirth,
Which, with its loud and clam'rous brawls,
Too oft has echoed in these walls;
But, if I can such feats restrain,
Shall seldom echo here again.
Pray let not that good man prevail
To swill yourself with sluggard ale:
But when you've sipp'd a glass or so
Of wine that makes the bosom glow,
Let him go booze his fav'rite liquor
With the exciseman and the vicar,
While I expect my rev'rend friend
Will, in the drawing-room attend."

The rev'rend Friend bow'd his assent,
And with a flirt the lady went.
The 'Squire who scarce had spoke a word
While dinner smok'd upon the board,
No sooner was the fair-one gone
But he assum'd a lofty tone.

BUMPKIN.

"Doctor, I hope you know me better
Than to suppose that I can fetter
My sports and pleasures to the will
Of that same tongue that ne'er lies still:
You saw what pretty airs she gave,
As if I were a very slave;
But, my good friend, as you were by
I did not chuse to look awry.
Nor would I wound your rev'rend cloth,
By rapping out a swinging oath,
Which, but from my respect to you,
I was full well inclin'd to do,
And would at once have brought her to.
Yes, she may toss her head and hector,
But she shall have a curtain lecture:
I'll make the saucy madam weep,
Believe me, ere she goes to sleep.
I married Mary for her beauty,
And faith I'll make her do her duty.
Pray tell me, friend, what means you took
When a pert speech or haughty look
Was darted at you from your wife,
And threaten'd matrimonial strife?"

SYNTAX.

"She never spoke a saucy word,
She ne'er an angry look preferr'd:

IN SEARCH OF A WIFE

Affection dwelt within her eye
And all her speech was harmony:
But let I pray that subject rest,
Nor wake the sorrows of my breast:
For here I came on pleasure bent,
To share your well-known merriment,
And find good humour and content;
My gloomy fancies to beguile
And learn from you a cordial smile.
Come, come, a foaming bumper quaff,
And let me hear you loudly laugh."

This counsel given in solemn measure,
Appear'd to check the 'Squire's displeasure;
But though his spirits ceas'd to flutter,
His pouting lips were seen to mutter.

At length the coffee was announc'd:
Again he swell'd, look'd big and bounc'd:
But when the bell was made to ring,
For well he knew who pull'd the string,
Another song he chose to sing.
"My worthy friend as you are here,
I in good humour will appear,
And since the meagre slip-slop's made,
I think the call should be obey'd.
But one glass more I must engage,
My present feelings to assuage,
Though, to speak truth, I'm always dry
When this same bev'rage meets my eye."

Now led by fragrance and perfume,
They pass'd into the drawing-room,
Which, from its bright display of flowers,
Might pass for one of Flora's bowers.

—Syntax enchanted at the sight,
Broke forth in language of delight.
"—When the Creator's works I view
And, wond'ring, the bright course pursue;
And from sublimest objects range
To most minute in endless change;
If in those works that meet the eye,
From sky to earth, from earth to sky,
He in the greatest stands confest,
Still is he greater in the least." [1]

Thus as he spoke, with ardent glow,
Of all the various tribes that grow
Or in the garden or the field,
Or which the rock or mountain yield,
From the wide spreading cedar tall,
To the low hyssop on the wall,
The yawning 'Squire devoid of thought,
With lazy stride the sofa sought,
The cushions cuff'd with all his strength,
And then laid down his listless length.
Madam grew red, and then grew white,
And gave her rosy lips a bite,
Which might denote an inclination
To gratify a rising passion:
When the Divine to turn aside
The rising burst of wounded pride,
Continued, with encreasing force,
The fervour of his sage discourse;
But as the lady lent her ear,
To what she was so charm'd to hear,
Poor Bumpkin with a snort and snore,
Roll'd from the sofa on the floor:

---

[1] Si l' Auteur de la Nature est grand dans les grandes choses, il est tres grand dans les petites.—J. J. ROUSSEAU.

IN SEARCH OF A WIFE

The servants did their master shake,
But he was not dispos'd to wake:
"There," said their mistress, "let him lay,
To pass another hour away.
Oh Doctor! ought I not to bless
My share of married happiness!
Is not this quite enough to shame me?
Nay, can you for my anger blame me?
Excuse me, but I scarce should weep
If this were his eternal sleep.
—Where the taste and tempers vary,
O what a folly 'tis to marry!
The greatest fortune will not suit
The gentle spirit with the brute:
Nor the fond, tender inclination,
With a mere instinctive passion,
Nor the affection of the soul
With the rude mind that claims the whole,
And will not share the kind controul.
—'Tis true I have a coach-and-four,
Whene'er I call it, at my door:
Or, as I please to take the air
Command the ponies to a chair:
And when I ride, I also see
The Beauty Mare reserv'd for me.
I decorate my drawing-room
With earliest flowers to breathe perfume,
And if I chuse, I have the power
Winter to clothe with vernal bower:
And if it should my fancy suit,
To taste in Spring the Summer fruit;
While my gay pride, may, to excess,
Enjoy the toilette's happiness.
I can make this old mansion gay,
With song or dance in any way

That my fine vanity may chuse
The neighb'ring circle to amuse.
All this you know, perhaps, but still
It does not my fond wish fulfil.
You, Sir, may ask, the question's fair,
What 'tis I want I do not share?
What is it I do not receive
Which a fond husband's bound to give?
That secret, Doctor, I'll impart:
I want what he has not—a heart:
Yes one, where tender feeling rules,
And warm affection never cools.
I want a character refin'd
Grac'd by a cultivated mind,
Where taste and science are enshrin'd;
With manners that from kindness flow,
Speech that is chaste, and thoughts that glow.
Failings e'en in the best must be,
But love would ne'er those errors see,
When it th' enraptur'd power possest
To nestle in a noble breast.
—On shaggy mountain's lofty brow,
Or in the woody vale below,
Or by the ocean's craggy side,
Believe me, I would rather bide,
With such a being by my side,
Than with stupidity to live
And all the show which wealth can give;
Though that show tempted me to join
A Booby's lasting lot with mine:
Such is my fate, for you must see
To whom false fortune coupled me."

The slumb'ring 'Squire now op'd his eyes,
Look'd round the room with dull surprise,

Then slowly rose and shook his head,
Call'd for a light and went to bed.

Mrs. Bumpkin.

"Since, my good Sir, what has appear'd,
Which you have seen as well as heard,
You must acknowledge my complaint
Doth ask the patience of a Saint."

Syntax.

"Excuse the liberty I take
When thus I most sincerely speak;
But that same virtue would confer
Perfection on your character.
O let me beg you to attend
To the kind counsels of a friend!
The die is cast, the deed is done,
The cord is fast that makes you one:
Though, if well order'd, I confess
I see no bar to happiness.
When I perceive the nat'ral state
Of reason in your married mate,
I would consent, in word and deed,
That you, fair Dame, should take the lead;
But then employ your better powers
To rule by sweets and not by sours.
Madam, the ancient proverb says,
Which words can never duly praise,
That one rich drop of Honey sweet,
As an alluring, luscious treat,
Is known to tempt more flies, by far,
Than a whole tun of Vinegar.
—Ask with kind words, he'll ne'er deny,
Give winning looks and he'll comply
With waken'd sensibility.

If you but smile and never frown
He'll shape his wishes to your own:
Nay, symptoms of obedience show,
Whether you do obey or no.
Thus blest with temper's cloudless ray
Your morrow will be like to-day.
O let him not perceive you rule,
Nor ever treat him like a fool;
Do not, at least, to others show,
If he be such, you think him so.
O ne'er again delight to tease him,
But look as if you wish to please him.
Check notions, that so idle prove,
Of Shepherds and Arcadian love:
Your active, well instructed mind,
To such vagaries should be blind,
Let not your fancy e'er refine
Beyond calm reason's fair design,
But leave to Misses of eighteen
The raptures they from Novels glean,
You surely have the means to bless
Your life with social happiness;
And O beware, you do not spoil
Your comforts with domestic broil!"

Mrs. Bumpkin.

"Doctor, I do admire your plan,
And I'll pursue it—if I can:—
But as so learn'd you seem to be
In all domestic policy,
'Tis pity you do not again
Assume the matrimonial chain."

Syntax.

"Madam, you've touch'd a tender string,
That doth to my remembrance bring

The heavy loss I have sustain'd
Of virtues ne'er to be regain'd.
My dearest Dolly was to me
What I wish ev'ry wife to be;
And since the darling saint is gone,
I feel it sad to be alone;
But still my doubts I cannot smother,
Of ever getting such another."

Mrs. Bumpkin.

"You have my happiness in view,
And I must feel the same for you.
I have a very pleasing friend
Whom to your thoughts I shall commend;
And, if my judgment does not err,
In form and age and character,
Dear Mrs. Hyacinth will prove
An object fit for you to love.
She in retirement's peaceful dell
Doth in her widow'd cottage dwell,
Though, if her thoughts to me are known,
She wishes to live less alone.
Her mind employs the quiet hours
In study, and in nursing flowers,
For, as I hope, you soon will see,
She has a taste for Botany;
And her delight as well as glory
Is in her gay conservatory.
Nor is this all—for you will find,
That with chaste manners is combin'd
A well form'd and accomplish'd mind.
At all events my friend may call
To make his bows at Tulip-Hall;
(For by that name the place is known
Which she is proud to call her own.)

While I its mistress will prepare
To give you a kind welcome there:
And much I wish that Heaven may bless
My friends with mutual happiness.
That flowers which sweetest fragrance breathe
May form an Hymeneal wreath,
With fairest hopes your life to crown,
When this fair Dame may be your own."
—The Doctor promis'd to obey,
And in high spirits more than gay,
He joyous kiss'd the lady's hand,
And bade her all his soul command.
—Brief was the evening's calm repast:
The time of rest arriv'd at last,
When the sage pass'd its balmy hours
In dreams of Hymen crown'd with flowers.

The morning came when a smart stroke
At chamber-door, the Doctor woke;
And strait, in rather serious mood,
By the bed-side 'Squire Bumpkin stood.
Syntax now rubb'd his eyes, amaz'd,
And on the intruding figure gaz'd;
Who lolling on an elbow-chair,
Began his errand to declare.

"—To wake you thus may be distressing,
But let me speak while you are dressing."
Syntax soon shook off his alarms,
Yawn'd wide, and stretching out his arms,
"Speak on," he said, "my worthy friend,
And I will to your words attend."

BUMPKIN.

"You must have seen, with half an eye
The kind of animosity,

In greater or in less degree,
That reigns between my wife and me:
And as you are a man of science,
On whom I have profound reliance,
Tell me the track I should pursue;
What to avoid and what to do,
When to controul it would be fit,
And when 'twere better to submit:
In short, that this great house may be
A scene of greater harmony.
I do not such a polish wear
As doth the exterior form prepare,
To rank among the dandy fools,
Who are gay fashion's fribbling tools:
But what I do should not provoke
Her saucy wit's sarcastic joke,
And, showing off her lively sense,
Make others laugh at my expence,
Of which she's sometimes too profuse,
But I think worse than rank abuse;—
For if in that she chose to stir
I fancy I could equal her.
But, to my friend, I here declare it,
I've sometimes said I will not bear it."

 Syntax as he his garters tied,
Thus with half-open'd eyes, replied,
"You have, all know, a generous heart,
That spurns the unmanly tricks of art;
Nor are you wanting to pursue
What common-sense holds forth to view,
And these short precepts you will find
The best directors of your mind;
Nay be assur'd, they will succeed,
To set you right in word and deed.

A sportsman knows 'tis to his cost
Who takes the wrong side of the post:
As on the course, so in life's stake,
You must agree to give and take:
To bear and forbear is a rule,
A lesson prime, in reason's school.
Try, as you can, your best to please,
And, when she that endeavour sees,
I'm sure she will no longer tease."
"—This is good preaching," Bumpkin
 said,
"For you well understand your trade.
That it is true must be confest,
And, faith, I'll try to do my best."·
—He kept his word, and so did she;
At breakfast all was pleasantry:
And thus, the gloomy season past,
'Twas hop'd the Halcyon time might last.

When Syntax rose to take his leave,
He said, "this counsel kind receive:
I do prefer it nothing loth;
And mind—*I give it to you both.*
—For trifles ne'er contest the field,
But rather struggle who shall yield.
Let but Affection bear the sway,
And you will struggle to obey:
That feeling ever checks the strife
Which tends to poison wedded life.
Call but affection to your aid,
And the tongue never will upbraid;
The heart is then a kind of Heaven,
Where ev'ry failing is forgiven.
Without it, sad is Hymen's reign,
And fortune's smiles are shed in vain:

O let but that the union bless,
And the sure boon is happiness."

   The Doctor now his way pursued
Through verdant dale and shady wood,
While he reflected on the scene
Of Hymen's joys, where he had been,
And rather doubted if again
He should receive the marriage chain.
"Patrick," he said, "how did you find
The place which we have left behind?
Had you kind hospitable fare,
In the domestic regions there?
And were you free and joyous all,
In butler's room and servants' hall!"
"Oh, as for those things," Pat replied,
"Plenty and joy do there reside:
But though I've travell'd kingdoms o'er,
I never heard such things before.
The lady doth a form display
But seldom seen in summer's day:
Nor, then the 'Squire, doth the sun
A finer figure shine upon;
And, in some way, I understood
From morn to night they're doing good.
The poor are never seen to wait
In vain attendance at their gate;
Nor pain nor sickness ever feel
The want of means to soothe and heal;
While children, ere they run along,
Are taught to know the right from wrong.
—But here, and please you, Sir's the bother,
They're kind to all but one another;
And scarce there passes on a day,
But they're engag'd in angry fray,

When, by her woman, I was told,
He's heard to growl, and she to scold,
Though, as she said, things might be worse,
For the grey mare's the better horse.
You may explain, Sir, if you please,
Such uncouth odds and ends as these;
But faith, to me it doth belong,
To shut my eyes and hold my tongue,
Unless you do the fancy take,
By way of joke, to hear PAT speak."

 Thus as they went, a coming storm
Did the sky's azure face deform,
Whose menace bade them look around
To where a shelter might be found;
And soon a pleasing cot was seen
Amid the hamlet on the green:
The honeysuckle flaunted o'er
The porch that stood before the door:
Nor did the ivy fail to crawl,
In spreading verdure, o'er the wall:
Away from the world's noisy din,
It look'd the seat of peace within.
Thither they did in haste repair
And found a smiling welcome there.
All look'd so nice, so clean and warm,
Within the comfortable farm,
When she appear'd, the way to show,
Whose household care had made it so.
The Dame with smiles, the Doctor greeted,
Desired his Rev'rence would be seated,
And did, with curtsying grace, prepare
The comforts of an easy chair;
Hasten'd his gaiters to untie,
And hung them at the fire to dry:

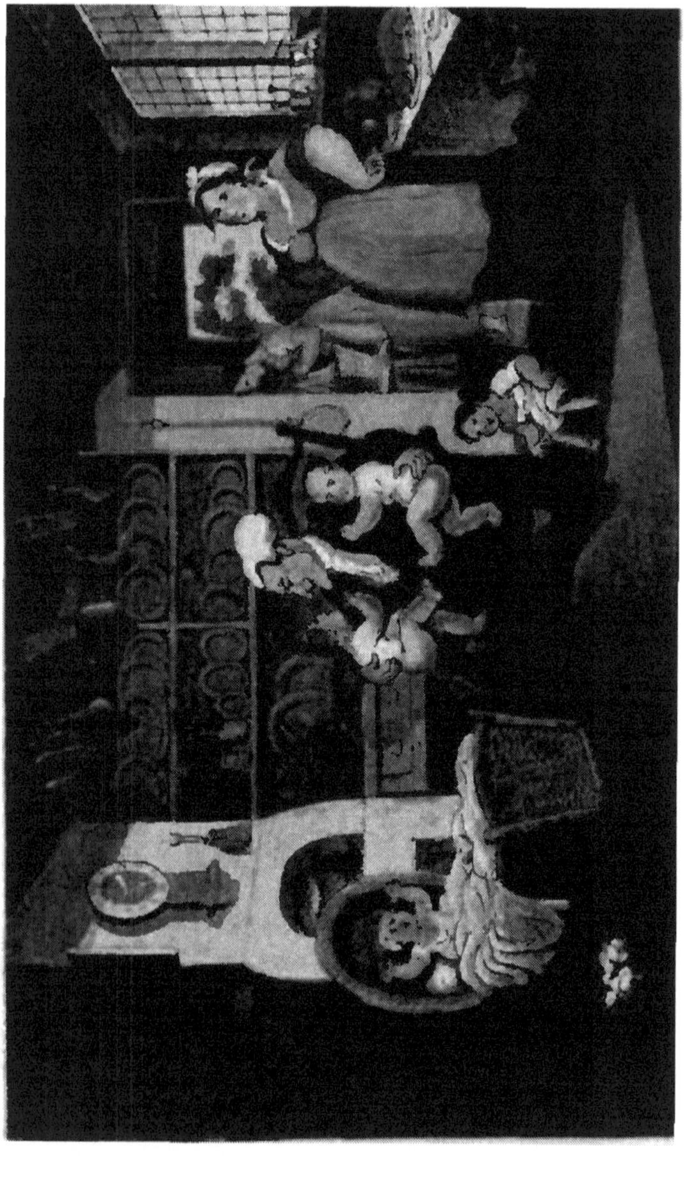

Then humbly hop'd he would receive
The entertainment she could give.
"There is a pye in oven baking,
There are hog's puddings of my making,
And no rich 'Squire, throughout the vale,
Can give a better cup of ale."
Nay, Syntax, e'en with well lin'd purse,
Might have gone farther and far'd worse.
"—I here," he said, "see children four,
Pray, Goody, have you any more?"
"Not yet, Sir, but, as I'm their mother,
I hope in time to give another;
Which I, it seems, begin to show,
As all who use their eyes may know."
"Well my good woman," Syntax said,
"I see one great command obey'd;
With that you piously comply:—
I mean —ENCREASE AND MULTIPLY."
—Himself and the good dame to please,
He took the children on his knees;
Then danc'd the urchins too and fro,
And sung as nurses often do.

Song.

Lullaby Baby, where shall we go,
   Lullaby Baby, up in a tree,
There we shall find a pretty bird's nest,
   For Lullaby Baby, for Charley and me.
For Charley and me, for Charley and me,
Lullaby Baby, for Charley and me.

Lullaby Baby, when the birds sing,
   Lullaby Baby, the cuckow and all;
Then we shall smell all the sweets of the Spring,
   With Lullaby Baby, and Charley and all.
   Charley and all, etc. etc.

Lullaby Baby in cradle doth sleep,
  Lullaby Baby the joy of its mother,
Who will soon if she doth a right reckoning keep,
  Give to Lullaby Baby a sister or brother.
  A sister or brother, a sister or brother,
  Give to Lullaby Baby a sister or brother.

"O Sir," she said, "you are too good
Thus to delight my pretty brood:
Not one of whom I e'er would give
Though the king's crown I should receive:
But, as you have a foot to spare,
Will you just rock the cradle there."

The Doctor was in full content,
When he perceiv'd a certain scent,
Which was not like the sweets of spring
That he had just been pleas'd to sing,
But the Muses' dainty noses
Are so used to pinks and roses,
That they know not how to tell
The nature of a vulgar smell.

"What mischief," Goody cried, "is brewing!
God bless the child, what is he doing;
And now, indeed, I do perceive,
As I must tell you by your leave,
The worm-pills which he takes, good Sir,
Have just begun to make a stir:
But still, I hope, no harm is done.
Come, sweetest babe, beneath the sun!"
And with the child away she run.

Into such laugh the Doctor broke
That made him look as he would choke.
And still, with ridicule at heart,
He sung and play'd the nurse's part.

Then lifted up his eyes to Heaven,
As if some blessing had been given.
"'Tis thus," he said, "Affection grows,
And thus the fond deceit bestows:
See what a mother will not do,
What will she not, when, to her view,
The fondling in her arms doth rest,
Or seeks the fluid from her breast.
'Tis the same glowing sense that burns
In father's breast, as he returns
From hardy toil, and doth repay
The labour of each passing day,
When on his knees an infant pair
Ask by their looks the kiss to share."

To give that kiss, to feel that glow,
JOHN enter'd with submissive bow,
Nor did he want the smiling grace
Of welcome on his ruddy face.

FARMER JOHN.

"An' please your Rev'rence here we are
Attending on our daily care:
I through my little fields must roam
While MARY governs things at home:
She is a kind industrious wife
The blessing of a husband's life;
And she, I doubt not, would agree
To speak with same content of me.
We, it is true, must have our cares,
Which mortal man in common shares.
The storm will sometimes blast the field,
And fruit-trees will refuse to yield;
While some incurable disease
Does on our flocks and cattle seize:

But then fair plenty comes again,
And flocks and herds adorn the plain.
Though whether it be good or ill,
We patient bear our maker's will,
Conscious we ought not to repine:
At least that's Mary's way and mine.
Thus time our checquer'd way beguiles,
I never frown, she always smiles;
For Heaven is kind, and, as you see,
Gives us both health and industry:
While it will be our constant care
These little bantlings here to rear,
In what our humble state demands,
The honest labour of their hands.
That they when our old course is run,
May toil and thrive as we have done.
—And now, I hope you will think fit
Of what we've got to pick a bit.
The oven does a pye afford,
The ale looks bright upon the board,
The liquor's good and brisk and humming,
And soon the puddings will be coming.
Here is not much to cut and carve,
But still I hope we shall not starve;
While I a grateful welcome give
To what your kindness may receive."
"No," Syntax said, "no never fear,
I stand a hungry figure here,
And thank you for your friendly cheer.
Besides your welcome gives that zest
Which turns a morsel to a feast;
That feast, my friend, I now enjoy,
Which satisfies, but does not cloy:
I'm as well-pleas'd with your bestowing
As I shall be where I am going.

To that point where the sun does rise,
From hence my present journey lies:
To-night, Sir *Stately Stirrup's* guest,
I hope at Stirrup-Hall to rest;
For his grave worship condescends
To number me among his friends."
" He may be proud," said John, " of you,
But what I tell you, Sir, is true,
His flock of friends is very few."

The Farmer now a pipe propos'd,
The Doctor on the offer clos'd;
And John who was not prone to balk
The fancy which he had to talk,
Continued with his rustic force
To paint the Knight in his discourse.

FARMER JOHN.

" He's a rum codger you must know;
At least we poor folk find him so.
By his grand politics and law
He keeps the country round in awe:
He thinks he knows, puff'd up with pride,
Far more than all the world beside:
But when did any body hear,
He for distress e'er shed a tear?
Or when did he a shilling give
A wife in labour to relieve?
Or when were seen the hungry poor
Receiving scraps before his door?
Nor does he think an orphan's blessing
To be a treasure worth possessing;
But warrants, staves, and mastiffs wait
To guard the approaches to his gate.
Yes, all his acts a tyrant show him
To all degrees that are below him;

But, let a man of rank go by,
He's ready in the dust to lie.
From me the laws ne'er find a breach,
I therefore keep without his reach;
Though if the hills which rise between us
Could from his paws for ever screen us,
O it would be a blessing found
By all the grumbling country round!
—You did not know his former wife:
She led the Knight a precious life:
That over-bearing haughty spirit,
Which he from nature does inherit,
She, whene'er she pleas'd, kept under,
With look of flame and voice of thunder.
He went abroad, 'tis true, to rule,
But home return'd so calm and cool,
That, but excepting form and name,
None would believe the man the same.
Nor has he ever yet denied
He bless'd the day on which she died,
And that he thought her fun'ral rite
Was not a very mournful sight.
But you must know, as I suppose,
For 'tis what all the country knows,
Ere a few months had pass'd away,
Old *Stirrup-Hall* again was gay
With marriage feast; and a young bride
Was seen to grace Sir Stately's side.
She, foolish thing, thought it a gay day
When golden ring made her a Lady;
But though she now precedence takes
Of 'Squires' wives around the lakes;
And though she doth a rank display,
Which time itself can't take away,
Yet she now finds, as 'tis well known,
She scarce can call her soul her own:

And as for gaiety or pleasure
'Tis dealt to her in grudging measure:
Nay, it is thought, as some folks say,
Who see and hear her ev'ry day,
That she oft wishes, though in vain,
She were Miss *Biddiken* again."

SYNTAX.

"I find, my friend, that you know more
Than I have ever heard before:
'Tis strange to me a swain like you
Can such a scene as this review;
And how it is you thus can pry
Into domestic history."

FARMER JOHN.

"On market-days, our bus'ness done
We sit and chat and have our fun;
And while we handle pipe and pot,
Our betters, Sir, are not forgot.
We hear the bad as well as good
In ev'ry farmer's neighbourhood,
And broach the news, with equal bounty,
From ev'ry corner of the County."

SYNTAX.

"Well, honest John, I ask you then,
What do you say of Sommerden?"

FARMER JOHN.

"Another cup before I speak,
And then I will the freedom take
To say what's in the country said,
Both of your heart and of your head,
Nor fear offence, though I speak true,
For good alone is said of you.

—You're call'd a man of deep discerning,
Fit for a Bishop by your learning;
Pious and good, yet very gay,
And that you on the fiddle play:
That in the pulpit you're a rare one,
And lay it on, and never spare one:
As for the bad you ne'er defend 'em,
But headlong to the devil send 'em:
Though, as the truth you wish to hear,
And what you preach you need not fear,
Folks say that you are rather queer."

Syntax.

"Give me your hand, my honest friend,
To more than this I'll ne'er pretend:
If it be true, I'm well content
Or for my life or monument.
I ask, indeed, no higher praise,
While Heaven may lengthen out my days;
Nor do I wish a better fame,
When nought is left me but a name.
Farewell, for the declining sun
Tells me, at length, I must be gone."
—After repeated kind caressing,
The Doctor gave the babes a blessing,
And having kiss'd the mother too,
"I feel," he said, "my thanks are due
For all I have receiv'd from you:
But keep in mind our Village Fair,
And who expects to see you there."

He trotted off, and ere the ray
Of parting Phœbus clos'd the day,
He had arriv'd in cleric state,
At Stirrup-Hall's old fashion'd gate.

IN SEARCH OF A WIFE

Pat quickly made the bell resound,
That echoed all the court around:
Nor was it long before the Knight,
In all due form appear'd in sight,
With "Glad to see you, how d'ye do?
I take this very kind of you:
And all within my friendly power,
You may command at any hour.
—'Tis well known what my life has been,
What my experienc'd mind has seen:
I've wrought my policy so nice,
That all come here to ask advice,
And, if your wish is to receive it,
You know who is prepar'd to give it."
They enter'd—when the talk began,
And the long conversation ran,
How the superior, leading, powers
Employ'd or misemploy'd their hours;
Who at the nation's helm preside;
What policy or statesmen guide:
That gross corruption sways mankind,
And int'rest base perverts the mind:
How bribes have blinded common sense,
Foil'd reason, truth and eloquence:
That industry the state maintains;
That honest toil and honest gains
Our fathers rais'd to power and fame;
That virtue boldly scoffs at shame,
And all, in selfish ends pursuing,
But scramble for the public ruin.
—At length Sir Stately condescends
To talk of neighbours and of friends;
The hist'ry of the County Quorum,
And what nice cases come before 'em;
While from his known superior skill,
They all submit them to his will.

"I've heard," he added, "what has past
Since I beheld your Rev'rence last:
I'm told that you have lost your wife,
Who gave such comfort to your life:
And here, perhaps, you're come to know
My thoughts of what you ought to do;
Whether your griefs at once to smother,
You should look round and get another,
Or on one pillow lay your head,
And rest you in a widow'd bed:
On that important point, I pray,
Hear what Sir Stately has to say.
You well may take my sage advice,
For, Doctor, I've been married TWICE;
And though to own it I am loth,
I've had but bad success with both.

"My first wife—'tis not very civil,
But, faith, she was a very devil.
She brought me money, brought me beauty,
But not a grain of nuptial duty;
For all she at the altar swore,
Did not remain the day-light o'er.
Old Stirrup-Hall she call'd her throne,
And here no master would she own:
Whether with tongue or threat'ning fist,
In vain I found it to resist:
At length, indeed, I thought it best,
If on my pillow I would rest,
To let fierce Madam have her way
And wield at home the sov'reign sway.
Thus I, who daily dealt out law,
And kept the neighbourhood in awe;
Though potent I abroad could roam,
Return'd to be a slave at home.

In short to check the daily storm,
I to her humours did conform;
And, to close all domestic riot,
I held my tongue and liv'd in quiet:
But she contriv'd with such keen art
To play the matrimonial part,
That all the country did agree
To throw the real blame on me:
Nay, I must own, the truth to tell,
Domestic things she manag'd well.
—Were she displeas'd, and we alone,
She would, but in a soften'd tone,
Sharply and glibly lay it on.
Yes, would hiss forth in viper's phrase,
Fool, upstart, and *et ceteras*:
But if a creature did appear
That could her observations hear
'Twas then my love, my knight, my dear.
Though 'tis long past, my ear still rings,
With her confounded whisperings;
And every fierce and taunting look
Are character'd in mem'ry's book.
—Five years and upwards I had been
Beneath this iron-scepter'd queen,
When fate most kindly set me free
From her domestic tyranny.
Though I a downcast visage bore,
As I my sable trappings wore;
Yet I must honestly confess,
So far from feelings of distress,
'Twas with a smiling heart I trod,
Behind her bier, the church-yard sod;
And silent thought, with tearless eye,
This was a happy obsequy.
But still I've prov'd without disguise,
Experience has not made me wise;

For ere another year was flown,
The Church made me and Lucy one,
Whom shortly my good friend will see
The mirror of stupidity.
The one so wise was, she must rule,
The other is almost a fool,
She, such a cold, unmeaning elf,
Thinks not for me, nor for herself,
While I am always on the spur
To think both for myself and her."

"Yes," Syntax said, "to me it seems
You've run into the two extremes;
Your mind, I think, had lost its force,
Or you'd have sought the middle course.
Your conduct, Knight, but seems to prove
Reason has nought to do with Love.
Philosophers have said, 'tis true,
And it may be applied to you
That Reason fails whene'er the dart
Of am'rous passion stabs the heart,[1]
Or when its secret pulses move
To beat time to the tune of love.
'Tis whim, 'tis fancy, or 'tis chance,
That joins us in the wedding dance;
Though some have thought a wayward fate
Commands or shapes the nuptial state:
By others an opinion's given
That marriages are made in Heaven;
Though much I fear you'll not agree
In that sublime Philosophy;
But 'tis a diff'rent case with me,
Who, from my sense of love's dominion,
Declare I join in the opinion,

---

[1] Nemo sobrius amat.—SENECA.

IN SEARCH OF A WIFE

That wives are known who do combine }
Some little spice of the divine ;
At least that was the case with mine.
Nor my fond hope shall I now smother,
That Syntax self may get another,
Who does those qualities possess
Which promise married happiness :
And as I do with candour view,
(I do not say 'tis so with you,)
The various causes which perplex
The marriage state and Hymen vex,
I think the husband frames the strife
In full proportion with the wife."

"You men of learning," said the Knight,
"Who in your closets strike a light
On life's so sombre mysteries,
And shape and paint them as you please ;—
You classic men, whose fancy gives
A colour to whatever lives,
To all our sorrows or our joys,
To what delights or what annoys,
Your fine-drawn, your high-flying sense,
Disdains our dull experience,
Which measures all things by the square,
And sees things as they clearly are ;—
If you my first grand wife had known,
Who, I thank Heaven, is dead and gone,
That she was fit, you would have said,
E'en to have shar'd the Thund'rer's bed,
A Juno she, and it appears
She would have box'd the Thund'rer's ears ;—
While, as I speak, you may divine,
She had the courage to box mine,
Nor will you think I do deplore
That she's box'd up to box no more.

And when you see the gentler grace
That now supplies Ma'am Barbara's place,
With flowers from your poetic tree
You'll deck her insipidity,
But still in vain, I think you'll strive
To make her tell you she's alive."

Thus as they talk'd the supper came,
And with it the insipid Dame.
" Insipid ? " to himself exclaim'd
The Rev'rend Sage, " how falsely nam'd ! "
If ever he beheld an eye
That beam'd with kindred sympathy ;
If e'er a smile on features play'd,
That a benignant heart betray'd ;
If ever rightly understood,
He saw a being fair and good,
He could those charming symptoms trace
In Lucy's manners, Lucy's face.
But amid this superior merit,
Which he believ'd she did inherit,
He saw at once an humbled spirit.
Nay, now he felt that he must own,
What he had heard from Farmer John ;
While in Sir Stately's voice and mien,
Ungracious speech or look of spleen,
Was but too plainly heard and seen.

The Doctor with good-humour'd chat,
And brisk remark on this or that,
Strove from the fair to get a speech,
But that was not within his reach ;
While all the thoughts he did display,
Could only draw a yea or nay,

With humble bend and silent grace,
By which he could no pleasure trace,
With sometimes an uplifted eye,
A hectic blush, or gentle sigh.
—The Doctor felt what all would feel
Who could another's thoughts reveal,
And saw that care's corroding dart
Was rankling in the virtuous heart;
While over-bearing power sat by,
Nor pitied patient misery.

   The supper o'er, the Lady gone,
(More than content to be alone,)
The Knight began, with bloated pride,
Both love and lovers to deride,
And in his warmth, declar'd a wife
Seldom improv'd the lot of life:
At least Miss Fortune, in her whim,
Had fully prov'd it so to him.
"I've told you, that my former choice
Gave me no reason to rejoice,
And the last gift of treach'rous Cupid
Is pretty, but she's very stupid.
—O Doctor, Doctor, ne'er again
Bind yourself round in marriage chain.
If in love's lottery you have tried
And gain'd a prize be satisfied,
Nor hope that fickle Fortune e'er
Will make you twice her favorite care.
—Ask not for beauty, it doth lay
Its nets of roses in our way,
When we are led by tint and shape,
Like Zeuxis' birds to peck the grape;
And 'stead of chaste affection's glow,
We find, alas, a painted show.

But if you are resolv'd to try
Once more a nuptial destiny,
Which my experience bids me say,
Is placing you in danger's way,
Think not I beg about the charms
That waken passion's soft alarms;
But let a fortune and sound sense
Determine the pre-eminence.
I know, my friend that you inherit
A portion large of manly spirit,
That you would ne'er be brought to speak
In humble tone of Jerry Sneak;
And so attach'd to learned lore,
Of which you have a treasur'd store,
That you would thus describe a wife:—
One who had such a view of life,
Between the vulgar and refin'd,
As suits the tenor of your mind;
With manners too of that degree
Which blends with Cleric Dignity:
And such a partner could you find
You to your fate might be resign'd.

" Nay, now I think, that I know one,
Our friend the widow *Omicron*,
Who may, if I conjecture right,
Give to your life a new delight.
She's known for that superior knowledge,
Which would do honour to a college:
Nay in a college she was bred,
Of which her father was the Head:
By a learn'd Dean she then was lov'd,
Who a fond, short-liv'd husband prov'd;
But left her, as she haply found,
His books with twice six thousand pound;

And, as her fortune I review,
Her house and household chattels too:
By letter I will recommend
The Doctor to this female friend.
—Think not my sage that I am prating,
Ovid's Epistles she's translating;
And that pursuit may seem to prove
The Lady somehow thinks of love.
Attack her, win her, wear her then,
And give new life to Sommerden!"

Thus did the lengthen'd evening pass,
Enliven'd by the cheerful glass:
But, as the Sage retir'd to rest,
Fair Lucy's silent charms possest
The fine warm feelings of his breast.
Whether th' inspired Doctor thought
Exactly as a Doctor ought,
Or whether fancy 'gan to play,
It is not for the Muse to say;
But Pat declares his Master said,
As he was stepping into bed,
"If but that loit'ring fellow Death,
Would just now stop Sir Stately's breath,
And set the charming woman free,
I'd ask her if she'd marry me.
No, never would I make a stir
To rule the house and govern her,
But should rejoice, throughout my life,
To yield me up to such a wife;
A crowing cock I should be then,
Though daily peck'd by such a hen."
Thinking on her he heav'd a sigh
In sad and pitying sympathy;
And seem'd as if about to weep,
Had he not fallen fast asleep.

At early hour the following day
Syntax proceeded on his way,
Until they reach'd a shady isle
Where all the gen'rous virtues smile,
Those virtues which had long possess'd
A mansion in NED EASY's breast;
Who here enjoy'd his tranquil lot,
By the gay, busy world forgot.
—NED in his early life was known
Through all the purlieus of the town,
And took, 'tis said, no common measure,
Of what the laughing world calls pleasure.
He also had a warrior been,
And many a bloody field had seen;
Had pass'd the salt wave o'er and o'er,
And swelter'd on the sultry shore;
Had bravely sought his country's foe
In vales of ice, on hills of snow;
True to his country, which he serv'd,
He ne'er from rigid honours swerv'd;
That honour was his brightest aim,
Nor has his life e'er lost the name;
But when peace gave the joyous word
To sheathe the sharp and blood-stain'd sword,
The soldier laid his trappings by
T' enjoy a life of privacy,
And sought the tranquil calm retreat
Of his retir'd, paternal seat,
Where, in sweet peace and rural pride,
The 'Squire, his father, liv'd and died.
Here NED with good, sound common-sense,
Health, mirth and ample competence,
Laughs at the busy world, and all
That fashion's votaries pleasure call:
Here all his various wand'rings cease,
Here all his labours rest in peace.

His mirth is pure, with harmless wit,
Nor is he shy of using it;
And though not bred in learned college,
He has a useful store of knowledge;
While cheerful, bounteous, frank and free,
He beams with hospitality.
Good-humour ever seems to cheer him,
And makes all happy who come near him:
His very name will oft beguile
A cheerless thought, and cause a smile.
Nay it is true that since he married,
Not one fond hope of his miscarried.
And that is rare, you must agree,
For wives, 'Squire NED has married three :—
Nor has, as yet, the growing train
Of boys and girls e'er caus'd him pain.

'Twas nine, as the clock struck the hour,
When Syntax reach'd the mansion door.
The swelling hills that rose around
Appear'd with sylvan beauty crown'd;
The lawns display'd a charming scene
Of waving surface cloth'd with green,
While the lake spread its waters clear
With glittering sun-beams here and there;
And many a white, expanding sail
Receiv'd the impulse of the gale.

SYNTAX.

"O Nature bright! how can it be,
When man beholds thy charms, that he
Can be insensible to thee!
Whene'er he casts his upward eye
To the vast, blue ethereal sky,
Or turns it to the wond'rous robe
That clothes the surface of the globe,

With all the expanse that man can see
In boundless rich variety
Of hill and dale, of plain and flood;
What by the mind is understood?
'Tis NATURE tells of NATURE's GOD!
—But still that animated thrush,
Which warbles in the hawthorn bush,
Though by instinct it is he sings,
Advances in the scale of things,
'Till reason doth the system close,
From which the World from Chaos rose.
Nay, there's NED EASY, in his way,
Teaching his growing boys to play,
To strike the ball, to guard the wicket,
In all the mystery of cricket:
Nor can I bravely blame the plan
At times to lay aside the man,
To seize the frolic, lively joy,
That turns the man into the boy!"

'SQUIRE EASY soon the Doctor spied,
When he approach'd and smiling cried,
"You as a learned man, I know,
Yes, you can tell me where and who;
But surely as my name is Ned,
In some old history I have read,
Of a wise people, where the rule,
Whether they were at home or school,
Ne'er did permit their youth to eat
'Till by some grave or active feat
Of mind or body, they had won
The privilege to pick their bone.
Who used to place the bread and cheese
On topmost boughs of lofty trees,
Nor ever suffer them to eat it,
'Till down their bows and arrows beat it;

Nor did they get a steak or tart,
'Till it was struck by sling or dart.
Nor will these boys their breakfast see,
'Till by some brisk activity,
Or studied lesson, they're prepar'd
To fix their teeth in their reward.
Hunger, by you know whom, 'tis said,
Will break through walls to get its bread,
And here my notion may be right,
That this same hunger may incite,
Of learning's loaf to get a bite.
—I, my dear Sir, make no pretence
To more than gen'ral *common-sense*,
Which, as fam'd *Pope*, the Poet, says,
A genius bright of former days,
Is 'mong the kindest gifts of Heaven,
And fairly worth the other seven.
When fine folks smile, I never mind it;
I take the world just as I find it,
Yes, yes, with all its odds and ends,
I know no foes, I love my friends;
And among them, it is most true,
Doctor, I'm proud to number you.
I'm an odd fish, but, to be free,
I'm not the only oddity:
Others there are, or I mistake,
Who make folks laugh about the Lake;
Where I remain, all tight and steady:—
But the bell rings, and breakfast's ready;
And sure I am Kate will rejoice,
From her good heart to hear your voice."
—Indeed her heart is well endued
With feelings that must make it good;
While she is sprightly, gay and free,
The flower of warm civility.

"So long," she said, "the time has been,
Since I beheld your precious chin,
That if I had the heart to scold you,
The house would be too hot to hold you.
But you, my friend, are wont to praise
My Edward's cot and all its ways,
And though some formal folks beshrew it,
You'll find it as you always knew it."
—Thus lively pleasantry prevail'd,
The Doctor's stomach never fail'd;
And though grave thoughts might intervene
At sight of this domestic scene;
Though his remembrance might be cross'd
By thoughts of her whom he had lost;
Yet the mild mirth that persever'd
His unresisting spirits cheer'd.

"At present," Easy said, "my Kate
Must on her house and children wait:
But in a busy hour or two,
She will reserve herself for you,
And try her best to make your stay,
Which we request for many a day,
A pleasant scene of grave and gay;
While we will have our friendly talk
Beneath the well-known filbert walk."
—Within that undisturb'd retreat
They sought a solitary seat,
When Easy the discourse began,
And thus the conversation ran.

Ned Easy.

"I have not hinted it before,
But truly I your loss deplore;
For though I'm not by nature taught
To court grave airs or solemn thought,

But rather mirth am prone to deal in,
Yet still, I trust, I have the feeling
In tales of real woe to join,
And make the ills of others mine:
Nay, that I'm anxious to relieve
All such as want, and those who grieve:
Though to my friend I freely own
Instead of answ'ring moan for moan,
I rather strive to laugh away,
The thoughts that on his bosom prey.
—To loss of friends we must submit
'Tis a wise power that orders it,
And when our joys he takes away,
His sov'reign will we must obey:
But who like you these truths can tell,
Who all our duties preach so well?
If weeping would relieve you, why
Let tears flow fast from either eye,
But to prevent a friend from dying,
Sure laughing is as good as crying.
—You've lost your wife—what's to be done!
Why, you may try to live alone:
If that won't do—what doth remain
To bring past comforts back again,
But without any fuss or pother,
To look about and get another;
And, ere a reas'ning hour is past,
To that same plan I'll nail you fast."

Syntax.

"But if Sir Stately tells me true,
'Tis the worst thing that I can do,
And now, Friend Easy, what say you?
Full-well you know the Lordly Knight,
Is fond to think that he is right,

Though from his matrimonial song,
He has been sometimes in the wrong."

NED EASY.

"Wrong do you say? I hate the brute:
He does not with my nature suit.
A brute he must be, who commands
Such softness with such iron hands.
Though as I may suppose, you know,
His first wife touch'd him up or so,
A woman of transcendent merit,
Who would not bend her lofty spirit
To a vain coxcomb's tyrant whim,
Which is so prevalent with him:
For *all* or *nought* he made the clatter,
So justice gave the fool the latter:
His boasting counsel throw aside,
And take NED EASY for your guide.
He cannot be compar'd to me,
With his *two* wives, when I've had *three*;
Nor shall I the base story smother,
Hen-peck'd by one, he flouts the other:
I do not mean to say he beats her,
But like a baby always treats her,
While I, though I have married been
So many years, at least sixteen:
Yes, I, with honest heart and hand,
Can now the *Dunmow Flitch* demand."

SYNTAX.

"Three wives you've had and, as you state,
Have chosen well in ev'ry mate;
Then tell me, friend, how you have done,
That Syntax may chuse such a one:
Whether it be from common sense,
Or fruits of sound experience,

IN SEARCH OF A WIFE

Or chance, or happy accident,
Your lot is one of such content;
That I may, lest the dames should flout me,
Know how, at least, to look about me."

NED EASY.

"Well then, believe me, I will tell
My honest, nuptial chronicle;
How all my diff'rent courtships thriv'd,
How I made love, and when I wiv'd;
'Tis a request I can't refuse you:—
At all events, it will amuse you.

"When I first sheath'd the shining blade,
And thought no more of my cockade,
Having escap'd *Bellona's* rattle,
And all the risques of bloody battle,
With limbs all sound, nor yet a scar
Which sometimes spoils a face in war;
Tho' dangers I ne'er fail'd to dare,
My eye-brows had not lost a hair,
And as the broad-sword work and lancing,
Had not cut short my grace in dancing,
I 'gan to think what I should prove
If Cupid drill'd me into love;
What guard I had against the dart
With which he might attempt my heart;
What store I had of vows and sighs,
And all those soft idolatries
Which wake kind looks in ladies' eyes.
But, while I these attentions paid,
MARG'RET appear'd, a blooming maid,
Who seem'd, I thought, well-pleas'd to hear
All that I whisper'd in her ear.
Egad, I ran at Miss full tilt,
But, in a week, she prov'd a JILT:

I courted with a chaise and pair,
Which seem'd at first to please the fair,
But soon the changeling gave me o'er,
For courtship in a coach and four.

"Then Charlotte came, a perfect grace
In outward form, but, on her face
Too oft was seen a scowling look,
Which my calm temper did not brook:
Nay, I had heard her scold her mother,
And seen her cuff her little brother.
She knew how to show off a charm,
In a most fine-turn'd hand and arm,
Which a known sculptor of renown
By modelling had made his own,
And us'd to show it as a piece,
That rivall'd the best works of Greece:
But then her fingers she could twist
Into a firm and fearful fist,
And much I fear'd, when married, she
Might lay that fine form'd fist on me.

"Maria next my bosom fir'd,
And fix'd the love which she inspir'd.
Her auburn locks were seen to break
In native ringlets on her neck;
Her smiles did to her face impart
The goodness of a tender heart:
In all her steps a grace was seen,
With winning words and gentle mien.
Oh, while she liv'd she lovely prov'd,
And never ceas'd to be belov'd!
—No, she ne'er left me in the lurch,
No, all she promis'd in the church
She did with fondest truth fulfil:
She studied and obey'd my will;

While her ne'er-failing kindness I
Return'd with grateful sympathy.
—These rosy hours, as thus they past,
Were far too blooming long to last:
Too soon she died—and jealous Heaven
Took back the Angel it had given.

"Two years pass'd on when my fond grief
Began from time to find relief:
Indeed I never thought again
To wear the Hymeneal chain,
'Till lively ISABEL appear'd,
Whose pleasant wit my bosom cheer'd,
And there inspir'd a subtle flame,
While her black eye confirm'd the same.
But as our intimacy grew
And I the lady better knew,
The gewgaws and the show of dress
Seem'd all her wishes to possess;
Nor could I happiness foresee
In her expensive gaiety:
So as I would not be outwitted,
I quietly the Lady quitted.
She threw about her lively flams,
And scatter'd round her epigrams,
Because NED EASY would not waste
His rents to suit her tonish taste,
But left the Miss, as I'm afraid,
To be an antiquated maid,
And to lead apes, O what a shame!
Where I, indeed, should blush to name.

"I next became the favour'd swain
Of sober and of gentle JANE,
Whom, with ten thousand pounds, I led
Well pleas'd to share my marriage-bed.

She could not boast the pride of beauty,
But then she felt the housewife's duty:
She was, indeed, a darling honey,
Who lov'd me well and sav'd my money:
In ev'ry useful, household care,
She bore a more than equal share:—
To scold the servant she was free,
But then she never scolded me.
Though she was careful, she was good,
And lov'd by all the neighbourhood:
Though foe to every vain expence,
She nourish'd a benevolence
Which aided the industrious poor,
And fed the hungry at the door.
At length she bore me children twain;
But, which I still relate with pain,
When procreative nature stirr'd
Its innate powers to give a third,
She, with the child, her new-born pride
At morning's dawn, ere evening died.

"Now discontent for once possess'd
The interregnum of my breast,
And sorrows, scarcely known, encrease
To trouble my domestic peace:
Hence calm reflection bids me try
In Hymen's chord another tie,
To soothe a widow'd father's care
And ease the toil which he must bear.
The widow HARLEY now I sought,
Who was an object as I thought,
Most fit, if not the only one,
To fill her place so lately gone;
Who would a tender mother prove
To babes whom I so fondly love,

IN SEARCH OF A WIFE

And, with a warm affection, be,
A kind and faithful wife to me.
Nay, as she had a little pride,
Whose wants her fortune ill supplied,
I thought, when I my hand should proffer,
She'd jump transported at the offer:
But, instead of grateful graces,
Smiling looks and warm embraces,
She, on venal interest bent,
A rascally attorney sent
To claim a hungry settlement,
With such conditions at the close,
That up in arms my passions rose;
When, to return his saucy airs,
I sent him, spite of all his prayers,
Four steps at once adown the stairs.
Thus the vile lawyer's head I broke,
And cast away the Widow's yoke.

"At length the best of girls I chose,
Whom my good friend the Doctor knows,
And knows I'm certain, to admire
As all a husband can desire.
Two more fine bairns my KATE has given,
The finest offspring under Heaven:
While she a parent is as good
To all the other growing brood,
As their own mother would have been,
Had she remain'd upon the scene.
Nor does she any thing to teaze me,
But always, always what will please me.
Whate'er I wish or do prefer,
Becomes an instant law to her.
By Jove I swear, it is no joke,
To please me she has learn'd to smoke,

And after dinner you will see }
A smoking trio we shall be }
Beneath a spreading beechen-tree: }
Where we our mod'rate cups will quaff,
There hear your pleasant tales and laugh—
And o'er the philosophic bowl
Let loose the language of the Soul."

SYNTAX.

"'Squire NED, your Hist'ry makes me feel,
As I must own, an added zeal,
Once more to try my future fate
In vent'ring on the marriage state.
Two Widows I have on my list,
And cannot you contrive to twist
Into the roll some female friend,
My hopes to feed, my chance to mend?"

Thus as he spoke, the welcome bell
The dining hour was heard to tell:
Mirth and good eating there prevail'd;
No stomach round the table fail'd;
And when with grateful pious zeal,
The Grace had sanctified the meal,
The smoking trio soon was seen
Beneath the tree upon the green.

NED EASY and the Doctor sat
With pipe in hand in usual state;
Thoughtless one look'd, the other wise,
With sleepy or with twinkling eyes,
While Ma'am the *Aromatics* blended,
To gain the scent which she intended,
As she would not her taste disturb
With plain Virginia's common herb:
She thought it would be vulgar joking,
T' acquire its perfume by her smoking.

—An iv'ry pipe with silver tip
She took within her rosy lip,
And, as she whiff'd her sweet lips moving
Set the exhaling vapour roving;
While o'er her brow it seem'd to wander
In a slow, curling, calm meander,
And, 'mid the branches of the tree,
Display'd a misty canopy.

    For a short time they silent sat,
Reflecting on they knew not what;
When 'Squire NED a glass propos'd,
And thus his friendly thoughts disclos'd.
"His Rev'rence does our counsel crave,
And our best counsel he shall have.
We know that he has lost his wife:
And, to renew the happy life
Which his connubial state enjoy'd,
His present wishes are employ'd;
And how his loss may be supplied
By finding him another bride,
Whose equal virtues may restore
The comforts he enjoys no more.
—Among th' unmarried fair we know,
And they may be a score or so,
Miss MARY CROTCHET strikes my view;
And now, my Cath'rine, what say you?
In all the fine, delightful art,
Whose sounds can raise or melt the heart,
We know full well the Doctor's skill,
And that may win her to his will."

MRS. EASY.
"We all admire his manly sense,
His learning and his eloquence,

His pleasant manners and his wit,
With such a way of using it;
And I should wish to recommend
So rare a husband to my friend:
But all these virtues will not do,
'Tis with his music he must woo;
I know his fiddle will do more
Than all his Greek and Latin lore.
No, no, he must make love in score;
Nay, whoe'er wins her, it must be
By his deep skill in harmony,
And by the power he has to prove,
That Music is the food of Love.

"There's not an instrument they say,
On which Miss Crotchet cannot play,
From the low bag-pipe's dismal hum,
To the all-martial kettle-drum:
Nay, in every branch of sound,
'Tis said her knowledge is profound.
For any thing that she may want,
She asks in a Cathedral Chaunt;
She suits her voice to every key,
And can discharge her nose in C.
Though when she lays her music by
To mix with gay society,
She's clever, elegant and easy,
With manners that are form'd to please ye.
Now if this scheme you should approve
To forward your designs in love,
Believe me, Sir, I'll not neglect
To tell her whom she may expect;
And in the warmest terms commend
The virtues of our valued friend:
Though, on reflection, I must own
They cannot be to her unknown.

I'm certain, Doctor, there's no danger
That she will treat you as a stranger."

Syntax.

"Well, if I do not gain my ends,
It will not be for want of friends,
And I must be completely stupid
If I do not find a Cupid
To aid me in the various views
Which now my pleasing hopes amuse:
For he's an Urchin that escapes
From Cyprian form to other shapes;
Who, Proteus like, his ends to gain,
Can diff'rent characters sustain.
For youth he has the poison'd arrow
That makes a bustle in the marrow,
And to the blood conveys the heat
That makes the am'rous pulses beat;
Which, with soft languor clothes the eyes,
The tongue with vows, the breast with sighs:
But for Miss Crotchet I must find
A Cherub of another kind,
Who, when he to his call engages
The grave Philosophers and Sages,
His garlands are not made of roses,
Nor does he scatter fragrant posies,
Their beauties with the season's past,
Their fragrance is not made to last,
But on his sober brow is seen
The lasting wreaths of ever-green.
Nay, when he wantons in the gay days
Of matrons and of learned ladies,
Another character he bears,
And other emblems then he wears.
For stocking blue resigns his bow,
And slumbers on a folio.

But in that near approaching hour
When I behold Miss Crotchet's bower,
I must call Cupid, as he chuses
To wanton with the Lady Muses,
To dip his cup and take his fill
Of the clear Heliconian rill;
And, to possess himself of hearts,
Play on the dulcimer with darts,
Or inflict all his secret wounds
By the soul-soothing pow'r of sounds.
But I've my doubts, I e'en must own,
Whether the lady may be won
By any int'rest I may prove
With this same treach'rous God of Love.
But should sage Syntax act the fool
And feel the shafts of ridicule,
He will, at least, have done no more
Than wiser men have done before;
And when no ill is thought or meant,
He'll join the laugh—and be content.
—To-morrow I shall see agen
The bow'ry scenes of *Sommerden*,
To pass a grave, reflecting week,
Before I my adventures seek;
Re-tune my voice with fara-diddle,
And practice on my welcome fiddle;
I then with spirit shall engage
In matrimonial pilgrimage."

As Syntax finish'd his discourse,
A friend was seen to quit his horse,
And soon Bob Single made his bows
First to the Lady of the house,
Who as she did those bows receive,
Curtsied in form and took her leave.

Then Easy's hand he warmly squeez'd,
And Syntax by both elbows seiz'd;
Nor did the smiling neighbour fail
To claim the jug that foam'd with ale.
—In lands and woods this 'Squire had clear
At least twelve hundred pounds a year,
And, in a sober state or mellow,
Was a good-humour'd jovial fellow:
Nor had he an unsocial name
But in the article of game:
And if he prov'd a vengeful foe,
It was the poachers found him so:
For, by foul means to catch a hare,
To ply a net or lay a snare,
Was, by this rigid sportsman's reason,
Deem'd a dire act of country treason,
Which he with more than vengeance due,
Call'd the law's rigour to pursue,
And punish'd, in his legal rage,
With cat-o'-nine tails and the cage.
—In all those noisy loyal greetings
Which are well known at public meetings,
He oft was heard to take the lead,
Was steady too in thought and deed,
Nor did reflection ever balk
A fancy for Stentorian talk:
In politics was always hearty,
Nor, for a moment, chang'd his party;
All private, petty views disdain'd,
And boldly Freedom's cause maintain'd.

Bob, to the middle age of life,
Had made his way without a wife;
Nor ever fail'd, with hackneyed gibe,
To rail against the married tribe,

And in warm language to prefer
The happier state of Bachelor.
Thus when he found the nuptial state
Had been the subject of debate,
With blunt remark and oft-told story,
Bob Single soon was in his glory;
And with important look, begun
To let his captious accents run.

Bob Single.

"I thank my stars that I am free:
I was not made for slavery!
Pardon me, Doctor, but the Church,
Has never got me in its lurch:
I should prefer the hempen string
To licence and a wedding ring
Quiet I love, and that word WIFE
Is but another name for strife;
—Our friend, Ned Easy, I allow,
Is better for the marriage vow;
For fortune somehow, as a whim,
Has work'd a miracle for him.
I'm forc'd to own that prizes three,
And rich ones too, I do agree,
He's gain'd in Hymen's lottery.
But this, I think, or friend or foe,
He is the bravest man I know;
For when I heard what he was doing,
I thought him running to his ruin;
I cried have mercy on him Heaven,
And may his folly be forgiven!
For travel all the kingdom over,
From the Isle of Sky to Dover,
The curious journey would be vain,
In hope to see the like again.

IN SEARCH OF A WIFE

—I know you'll argue that a nation
Exists alone by population:
That I'll acknowledge to be true,
Though I could add a word or two
To what is said by state physicians,
And niddle-noddle politicians:
I reason but from what I see,
That more or less, the stern decree
Of nuptial bonds is misery.
Exceptions, I was taught at school,
Are found to rise from ev'ry rule;
But such exceptions, I could prove,
Are rare in Grammar rules of Love.
I'm sure that I could name a score,
Aye more than that, yes, twenty more,
Who in their wives have so miscarried,
They scarce have smil'd since they were married.
—There's BILLY HUMBLE will not own
That he detests his bouncing Joan:
How oft that *Jerry Sneak* appears,
With smiling face and well pull'd ears,
When with soft words and fondling kiss,
He talks of matrimonial bliss;
While all, who know the coward, know
He scarce dare look, or speak or go,
But as in form, or mode, or measure,
She pleases to make known her pleasure.
I saw the booby t'other day
As he was pacing on his way
To fetch a doctor for his wife,
Whose illness might affect her life,
Nay he insisted he should cry
For a full week, if she should die;
And on this errand full of love,
He went as slow as foot could move.

His long, lank face, by home-bred wars,
Look'd red with scratches and with scars,
Which he with stamm'ring tongue complain'd
From his bad razors were sustain'd:
I laugh'd to hear his barefac'd tales :—
The razors were his spousy's nails."

The Doctor now impatient grown,
Of all he heard 'bout Jack and Joan;
With grave looks and sarcastic twang,
Thus put a stop to Bob's harangue.

Syntax.

"I've heard these stories o'er and o'er,
You know it Bob, and many more;
I wish you'd tell us something new,
And what is better, something true:
Not this poor cant, so stale, so dull,
That may come forth from any scull.
Excuse me, but it makes me sick,
Because I think it is a trick,
That men the marriage state deride
Some folly of their own to hide,
When in a wife they have miscarried,
And some low vulgar baggage married;
Some black-eye'd Moll, or rosy Nan,
Some priestess of the dripping-pan,
To whom malicious Cupid gave,
Such wond'rous powers to enslave,
That e'en a 'Squire of good estate
Could not resist his am'rous fate,
But still afraid that fate to own,
And bent to keep the rites unknown,
He bears disguis'd the sturdy bride,
To secret vale or some moor-side,

Where he may to his deary go,
And none the am'rous parley know.
Then to delude suspicion's eye
From looking after mystery,
His blust'ring censure does not fail
Against the marriage-state to rail;
Laughs at all husbands, wives abuses,
And no occasion e'er refuses
To treat with scorn the wedded vow,
As you, BOB, have been doing now;
Talks all the scandal that he can,
Then steals away to MOLL or NAN,
In some sly corner to improve
The unknown joys of wedded love.
—Such is the zeal I've known to stir
An unsuspected bachelor,
'Till some unlook'd for strange event,
Or from neglect or accident,
Or the keen, watchful, prying eye
Of envious curiosity;
Or the good dame's impatient pride ⎫
To draw the cruel veil aside, ⎬
Which did her real station hide, ⎭
Display'd at length the hidden plan,
And brought him forth a married man.
A nine days' wonder, it is true,
He then appear'd to public view,
Join'd in the laugh, left off his prate
Against the matrimonial state,
And now of Benedicts is found
The happiest all the country round.
—Thus have I known a cunning hen
Leave her domestic noisy pen,
And seek the covert of a bush
Where all was quiet, all was hush,

There lay her eggs, unheard, unseen,
Beneath th' o'er-shadowing foliage green,
'Till in due time the bird appears
Cackling aloud her hopes and fears,
Around her chirping, flutt'ring, picking,
A brood of unsuspected chicken;
Thus to the cot, as 'twere by stealth,
Bringing a troop of feather'd wealth.
—And who can tell, but, some years hence,
When time has broken down the fence
Of your reluctant awkward shame,
Forth from her covert the fair dame,
Who dares not yet avow her name,
If such an one by chance should be—
Excuse my curiosity—
May your long wedded mate appear
With little *Singles* in her rear!
Then bells will ring and music play,
And all your villagers be gay,
To celebrate your wedding day,
Full ten years since the deed was done,
When Parson *Slyboots* made you one.
How I should joy the day to see
When, cur'd of your vain heresy,
You should be Hymen's devotee.
I know I've read, but when or where,
Needs not at present be my care,
And I am ready to allow
Tricks may attend the nuptial vow,
That marriage, as by some profess'd,
Is but a money job at best,
That cold compliance may be sold,
That wav'ring hearts may be controul'd—
But love's beyond the price of gold.
And now my jovial, jeering friend,
Do to these wholesome truths attend!

How great the good were they imprest
On early manhood's glowing breast;
And, spite of you, gay noisy tramplers,
Misses should work them on their samplers.
—Those who true love have ever tried,
(The common cares of life supplied)
No wants endure, no wishes make,
But ev'ry real joy partake:
All comfort on themselves depends,
They want not power, nor wealth, nor friends:
Love then hath ev'ry bliss in store,
'Tis friendship, and 'tis something more:
Each other ev'ry wish they give;—
Not to know love—is not to live!"

   Syntax, now smiling, fill'd his glass,
Then bade the bright decanter pass,
And on the ruby juice intent
Gave this congenial sentiment:
"May Hymen with fresh wreaths be crown'd,
And fusty bachelors be drown'd!"
—Bob's visage gloom'd with discontent,
His colour came, his colour went:
Whether it was a fancied joke,
Or truth prophetic Syntax spoke,
Old faithful Time would not forbear
In its due season to declare;
But by Ned Easy it was thought
The net was spread, when Bob was caught,
And that a picture had been shown
Which conscience told him was his own.
"Doctor," he said, "I must agree,
You much too learned are for me;"
Then fill'd the cup with ample measure,
And gave a frown that mark'd displeasure;

Pull'd the bell-rope with all his force,
And bade the servant bring his horse:
But though invited much to stay,
He grumbled *No*—and went his way.
—Syntax exclaim'd, "O let him pout,
I think that we have found him out:
O what a bursting of the bubble
To see *Bob Single* carry double!
Though now in other view so zealous,
I warmly hope to hear him tell us,
That life no higher joys can prove
Than those which flow from wedded love."

In friendly chat the evening pass'd,
Sleep's balmy season came at last;
When *Easy* said, "Here take my hand,
My heart, you know, you may command:
Such as it is, it ne'er beguiles
With flattery's deceitful smiles.
If you return to Keswick's side,
With a kind, gracious, pleasing bride,
I shall, with truth unfeign'd, rejoice
And loud congratulating voice;
But should your varying suits miscarry,
Should it not be your lot to marry,
And you might sometimes wish to roam
From your too solitary home,
Here you will find your friend NED EASY,
Ready to do his best to please you."
—Syntax return'd the grasping fist,
And with due grace the lady kiss'd,
Then sought the pillow's welcome powers
And slept through night's refreshing hours.

On the next morning, when the sun
His daily course began to run,

IN SEARCH OF A WIFE

The Doctor took an early flight,
In hopes to see his home at night,
Up to the hill he now ascends,
Then to the vale his way he bends,
Enjoys his meal at mid-day hour
Beneath a cot's inviting bower,
O'ershaded by the mantling vine,
And sweet with flow'rs of eglantine.
Pregnant with matrimonial dreams,
And flatt'ring fancy's thousand schemes,
He had beguil'd his sultry way,
When, at the misty close of day,
He reach'd the door he call'd his own,
But sigh'd to find himself alone.

Old Marg'ret hop'd that he was come
In health and better spirits home;
With kind attention did dispose
Her glasses on her peaked nose,
To see what signs his features bare,
Of calm contentment or of care,
But the good dame saw nothing there;
No cheerful aspect there was shown,
To call forth pleasure on her own.
—She told him all the village news,
As in his chair he chose to muse;
While he laid out where he had been,
What he had heard, whom he had seen,
And, wheresoe'er his face appear'd,
The welcomes which his bosom cheer'd.
But now the manor-house was left,
And for some months would be bereft
Of those warm friends who never fail'd,
When his free spirits were assail'd,
Since Fate, with Happiness at strife,
Had robb'd him of his darling's life,

To pour, by ev'ry friendly art,
The balm of comfort in his heart.
Thus while Madge sought his night's regale,
With soothing pipe and sparkling ale,
"O it will never do!" he said,
"The social power must be obey'd;
Such joy to hear a female tone,
I'll marry—I'll not live alone:
I'd sooner wed the first I see,
Though old and ugly she should be,
Than live in taciturnity.
Nay, ere another week is o'er,
I will begin th' important tour,
Nor e'er return, if I have life,
'Till I have found another wife!"

CANTO XXXV

WHAT is a Coxcomb?—'tis a fellow
A kind of dashing Punchinello,
That does his best attractions owe
To glitter and to outward show!
Nor is it to the form confin'd,
For there are Coxcombs of the mind,
And, perhaps, fairest ridicule
Rests with a better right and rule
Where the young man, just come from college,
With slight bespatterings of knowledge,
Does the grave attention claim,
That's due alone to learning's name;
Than where he in life's early vigour,
With glowing cheek and striking figure.
And all those spirits that give wing
To the blooming hours of spring,
Asks of vain Fashion's various art
Those gay attractions to impart;
Those trappings of exterior show,
Which catch the eye and form the beau.
—The real worth, the sterling good,
Require, to be well understood,
Reason, reflection, piercing sense,
And, above all, experience;
While what the surface may display
To gen'ral gaze, in open day,
Claims little but to see and hear,
A ready eye, an open ear.

Syntax well knew that what gave birth
To knowledge and to inbred worth
He could unfold with sure reliance,
And set all doubtings at defiance,
Nor did he fear a search to stir
In quest of real character;
But still he thought that something more
Than moral charms and learned lore,
Something that's sprightly, gay, gallant,
Must deck his journey militant:
"For," he exclaim'd, "in this same Tour
I do foresee, nay I am sure,
What obstacles I shall endure!
I almost tremble to recount them,
But then how glorious to surmount them.
I must a diff'rent course pursue
From all that I've been us'd to do;
My habits I must lay aside,
And cocker up my mind with pride;
Feed my calm fancy with a treat
Of what the world may term conceit;
For I shall never gain my ends,
With all the flattery of friends,
Unless I mend my awkward paces
And gain the favour of the Graces.
In common visits I could do,
But I'm to visit and to woo:
I may my flatt'ring unction ply
To please a lady's vanity;
But then do I possess the art
To play the humbug with the heart?

"The Dame who 'midst the fragrance lives,
That her conservatory gives,
Will ne'er allow tobacco's fume
To vapour in her drawing-room:

IN SEARCH OF A WIFE

I fear Ma'am Tulip, whose fine eyes
Are us'd to nature's richest dyes,
Which, from the morn to night, she sees
On flow'rs and plants, on shrubs and trees,
May with a sudden shriek start back
When she beholds my dingy black:
My speech then must be rich with flowers,
As her own aromatic bowers;
And I must bow and I must bend,
Ere to her favour I pretend;
And I must tell her she's as fair
As any of her lilies are.
If I should dare to snatch a kiss,
While I taste th' ambrosial bliss,
The loves to which the plants are prone,
And Dr. Darwin's verse has shown,
I must implore to be her own:
I must implore to let me hope
That I may be her Heliotrope,
And in return that she may be
A smiling Heliotrope to me.
But I must never say or sing
That the fine season is the spring;
Though after all, I fear she'll find
That I have left May-day behind;
That I am, what she does not want,
A stout, tho' but autumnal plant;
And much I fear I shall not prove
That autumn is the time for love:
However I will do my best
And to my stars must leave the rest.

"Still, on my way new doubts, I find,
Are ever springing in my mind:

Whether with comment or with text,
I feel how I shall be perplex'd,
Whene'er the learned dame I see,
The mirror of philology.
She has just pass'd the spring of life;
So far she'll suit me as a wife;
But to my hopes O what a blow
If I should dare to tell her so!
For 'tis her wish, as it appears,
To sink at least some saucy years,
And therefore *beautiful* and *young*
Must be familiar to my tongue!
For surely I've too much discerning,
If I should think mere praise for learning
Would bribe her glowing heart's consent,
However deck'd with compliment:
If I could brush up to her door
With liv'ried train and coach-and-four,
I then of love might truly speak,
And tell my Cyprian tales in Greek.—
But much I fear, my simple guise,
Will not attract the widow's eyes;
The way to favour I must find
By the exertions of the mind,
And by the sentimental art
Make out a passage to her heart.
And if I can the way discover
To be just smil'd on as a lover,
I'll treat this *Lady Omicron*
With *Ovid* and *Anacreon*,
And by those am'rous poets' fire,
I may her classic warmth inspire:
Ill-fortune then alone will hinder
My scatt'ring sparks upon her tinder;
And waking feelings which may move
Her bosom to contemplate love.

"As to Miss Crotchet, I must try
To work her into harmony.
The poet and historian tells
Music, that by its powerful spells,
Has been a source of miracles;
And I may hope without much stir,
To work a miracle on her,
If such it be, by music's art
To tickle an old maiden's heart.
—At all events I'll be as fine
As doth become a sound divine;
New clad, new hatted and new wigg'd,
With all becoming order rigg'd,
In that due figure to appear
Which suits the views of this career,
Whose final hist'ry will display
The colour of my future day."

Thus did he reason, thus he thought,
Then into use his fiddle brought,
And all his tender, melting airs
To win Miss *Crotchet* he prepares;
Then turns at times his curious eye
To scientific botany,
Which might prepare him for his call
And welcome kind at Tulip-Hall;
And thus by various means improve
The ways he plann'd of making love.

In the mean time he stroll'd about,
At farm or cot popp'd in and out,
And, with kind condescending glee,
Chatted with those he chanc'd to see.
One morn, as in the church-yard walking,
He to himself was calmly talking,

While Mat, the Sexton, sung a stave,
Half in and half out of a grave;
He was saluted by a dame,
And Cath'rine Horner was her name;
On whom, long past her early youth,
Old Time had work'd with rankling tooth:
Her wrinkled cheeks, so lank and dry,
Form'd channels for each wat'ry eye,
And on her chin the curling hair
Was thinly sprinkled here and there.
With age she was completely shent,
Her knees with tott'ring weakness bent,
And on a young man's arm she leant;
When thus she to the Doctor spoke,
In tones between a squeak and croak:
"I hope my suit may not miscarry;
I am to ask you, Sir, to marry."
His Rev'rence then, with scornful eye,
Began this curious colloquy.

Syntax.

"To marry?—whom? you doting fool!
What's got into your brainless scull?"
Th' old woman, striving to display
A bashful look, begg'd leave to say
"I meant not, Sir, to give offence
Unto your honour's reverence:
I mean no harm, as I can see,
When I ask *you* to marry *me.*"—
Now Syntax, had he seen a ghost,
Could not have look'd more terror-crost,
"What means the witch?" he stamping said,
"Or has your old age turn'd your head?"

M. H. "I've reach'd, 'tis true, my latter season,
But still, I hope, I've kept my reason;

IN SEARCH OF A WIFE

I cannot be an idle prater
If I but seek to follow nature:
I only wish you'd marry me
To the young man whom here you see;
And I declare as I'm alive,
I was last week but sixty-five.
I know I ne'er was much a beauty,
But honest Jack will do his duty;
And why should I withhold consent,
If I'm well-pleas'd, and he's content?
I know that many silly folk
Will turn grave things into a joke,
But where's the joke in this connection?
He gains support, I gain protection;
And let them laugh, when they shall see
That he has made a fool of me.
The girls may scoff, but they'd be glad
To have for sweethearts such a lad.
If I told all that I could tell "—

Syntax.

" If you were quiet, 'twere as well.
Sexton, I now must trust to you
What with these people I'm to do."

Sexton.

"An' please you, Sir, I know the story
Of this same pair who stand before you:
And though I feel I am but dull—
One is a knave and one's a fool:
Her cottage, that's by yonder wall,
He wishes to be his—that's all.
Besides 'tis known that Mother Horner
Has gold and notes in some sly corner,
And when that he has nos'd them out,
The Raff will make them fly about:

Though young he is a sorry sot,
Her little all will go to pot;
If he's permitted to deceive her
He soon will to the parish leave her.
I know the boy from five years old,
Saucy and impudent and bold:
When than that stone he was not higher
He was a most notorious liar;
And I must own I should be loth
To take his word upon his oath;
This leg of mine 'gainst that dead bone
I'll lay, that he's not twenty-one.
Always so wicked, and so wild,
'Tis said he's Farmer Fatgut's child,
For he maintain'd him while he liv'd,
And his tricks oft the old man griev'd.
He has been caught in laying snares
For catching 'Squire Worthy's hares,
And now with artful, am'rous fuss,
He's laid a snare for that old puss;
And, if not stopp'd in what he's doing,
He'll lead the old fool to her ruin;
For if he could, ne'er mind the sin,
He'd eat her flesh and sell her skin."

Again the old dame rais'd her voice,
"Pray," said the Doctor, "cease your noise,
Or else I fear you'll wake the dead,
Beneath the ground whereon you tread."

The Sexton once more stopp'd his trade,
And spoke while resting on his spade:

"Your Rev'rence, please you, need not fear,
She'll recollect who's sleeping here:

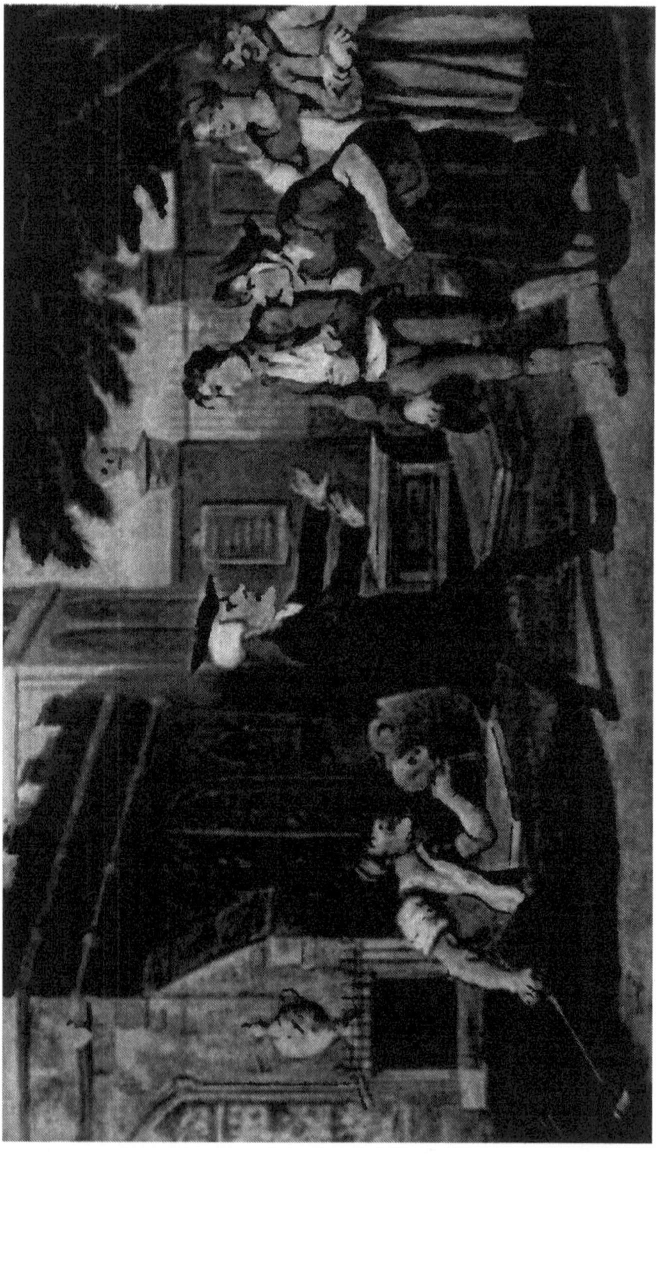

'Twas one who gave her many a thwacking,
To punish her foul tongue for clacking.
Persuade her that her tongue would wake
Old Simon, and she ne'er would speak.
I knew old Simon Horner well,
I dug his grave, I rung his knell,
Nay, well I know this is the spot
Where his remains were left to rot;
And I do think, or I'm a fool,
That this is honest Simon's scull;
And while I'm shov'ling 'mong these stones,
I bring to light his mould'ring bones.
Look dame and see how he is grinning,
To keep his wanton rib from sinning."
"Have done," the Doctor said, "have done,
Matthew this is too solemn fun;
If she will wed, why I must wed her,
And let deriding folly bed her.
I cannot marry them to-day,
So quickly send them both away."
—Jack made appearance to resist,
Clench'd both his hands and show'd his fist,
When the bold grave-man, at the meeting,
Gave the rude clown so sound a beating
That he forsook his hop'd-for bride,
While with his spade the conq'ror plied,
Stroke after stroke, the seat of shame,
Which blushing Muses never name,
And drove him, bellowing as he fled,
From out the region of the dead.
Th' affrighted dame, pale and down-hearted,
To find that she was thus deserted,
Mutt'ring revenge, and swearing too,
Which she was sometimes apt to do,
While hobbling o'er sepulchral stones,
Was pelted by her husband's bones,

And Matthew chose to let her know
Whose bones they were at ev'ry throw.
And thus she pass'd amid the jeer
Of all who were assembled there,
'Till of her cot she turn'd the latch
And sought the shelter of her thatch.

Syntax, half smiling, said, "This tale
Will long be echoed through the vale;
And many here will lie and rot
Before the story is forgot."

Time passes on, whate'er our schemes,
Our waking or our sleeping dreams,
Whether life's pleasure or its pain
Join in our course or form the train;
And it ran on until the hour
Call'd Syntax to th' appointed Tour:
Nor had he ever yet been seen
As to outward form and mien,
In all that gives exterior show,
So near what might be styl'd a beau,
As when he bade his home adieu
With one great object in his view,
To take for better or for worse
Heav'n's best of gifts or direst curse,
Which adds a smile or frown to life,
In the fix'd image of a WIFE.
All things were in fit style prepar'd,
With his known valet for his guard:
Well-curried Punch the Doctor bore,
Which PAT bestrode in Former Tour;
While he a farmer's gelding rode,
Of strength to bear the weighty load:
For prancing Phillis now was gone
To canter through a honey-moon;

And Syntax hop'd to see the day
When Punch would trot the self-same way.
—The journey's secret had been kept,
And while each curious tattler slept,
At early dawn, in tranquil state,
The Doctor pass'd the village gate,
Look'd cheerful, nay seem'd quite delighted,
In hope his pains would be requited.

In our life's chase what various game
Becomes the mortal huntsman's aim!
And then, with what discordant views
He that variety pursues!
They, who with independence bless'd,
And by no urgent wants oppress'd,
Who range at large and unconfin'd,
Free as the impulse of the wind,
Are often driven to and fro
By the various gusts that blow,
Unless calm reason checks their force
And keeps them in their steady course.
The passions are of life the gales;
Then keep the helm and watch the sails,
And with a clear and steady eye
Look to the haven where you hie.
"Nay ought I not," thought our Divine,
"To look to that which may be mine?
It seems, indeed, a pretty port,
Where Cupid may, perhaps, resort,
And Learning with the Graces three
Is said to live in harmony;
And who knows it may be my fate
To nestle there and change my state!
Its Mistress I've ne'er chanc'd to see,
Nor have her eyes e'er look'd on me,
Or my originality.

It is not that my form pretends
To dash at matrimonial ends;
'Tis by my tongue I must succeed,
'Tis that must do th' important deed:
I must depend on classic vigour
To give allurement to my figure;
And, watching her coquettish art,
Make my way boldly to her heart.
'Tis not by canting or by whining,
Or a long course of undermining,
That this fine fort can be obtain'd;
By sudden storm it must be gain'd.
Throw out false colours to her eye,
By weavings fine of flattery;
That she those weaker parts may show
Which will not stand a sudden blow.
If thus my powers should succeed
'Twill be a more than glorious deed;
And if I fail 'twill be no more
Than many a one has done before:
E'en heroes of the first renown,
Have had their hopes all tumbled down,
But then they did not strive in vain
Bravely to build them up again,
While persevering ardours bless
Their final darings with success.
Thus cheer'd by hope, my prospect's fair,
But while for struggles I prepare,
I snap my fingers at despair.
Of these so tempting fair-ones three
One will be full enough for me;
And my work must be idly done
If I do not secure that one—
And if dispos'd to be as kind
As the old dame I left behind:

IN SEARCH OF A WIFE

If I could find a Widow Horner
Wealthy and willing in a corner,
Well-looking and dispos'd to cooing;
O it would save a world of wooing!
And then I should re-visit home
Without another wish to roam."

Thus half in earnest, half in joke,
He in soft, mutt'ring whispers spoke.
—Of saunt'ring folk he would enquire
The name of ev'ry village spire,
Who was the Parson, who the 'Squire;
Whether the one his virtues prov'd
By such good deeds as made him lov'd,
And if the other did excel
In the first art of preaching well.
Nor did he ever fail to speak
With those he chanc'd to overtake;
And even had they nought to say
He was as well content as they;
So that they did well-pleas'd appear,
And give his words a list'ning ear.
'Twas thus he fail'd not to beguile
With pleasant chat the ling'ring mile.

Phœbus his course had almost run,
And soon would put his nightcap on,
Thus to prepare him for his nap
On the soft down of Thetis' lap,
When the embower'd spot was seen
Of which Ma'am *Omicron* was Queen.
—A chance companion on the road,
Who liv'd not far from her abode,
And happ'd to know the Doctor well,
Propos'd her mode of life to tell.

The Doctor too was glad to hear,
And op'd an interested ear.

"In this fair Lady are combin'd
The beauties of the form and mind:
She's rich withal and has withstood
Five years of tempting widowhood,
When many a suitor, but in vain,
Has strove her favour to obtain,
The soldier bold, the dashing 'squire,
Have hop'd to wake the amorous fire;
Beaux of various sorts and size
Have thought to bear away the prize;
But she, as it is said, has sworn
She ne'er to Hymen would return,
Unless the saffron-mantled power
Would join her, in his roseate bower,
To one with ancient learning fraught,
With all that modern science taught,
And in whose talents might be trac'd
The seeds of genius and of taste.
For one endued with such a mind
She'd leave exterior grace behind:
A scholar and a virtuous sage,
Whate'er his shape, whate'er his age,
Would her discerning heart engage.
A witty, a deform'd *Scarron*
She would prefer, like *Maintenon*,[1]
To all that superficial race
Who know no charm beyond the face,
And are enchanted by the plume
That waves in Fashion's drawing-room."

---

[1] The celebrated *Madame de Maintenon*, afterwards the secret wife of Louis xiv., espoused, in the bloom of her beauty, the infirm and deformed, but eminently witty *Scarron*.

Syntax this question then preferr'd :
"Think you that she will keep her word?"
When he was answer'd frank and free,
As such enquiries ought to be:

"My understanding's too refin'd
To fathom a fine lady's mind,
I cannot know and do not care
What whimsies may be passing there,
For my best half doth never own
A thought that is to me unknown.
A fond and amiable she,
As frank as honest heart can be ;—
But hear the best authority.
—The Widow's Rector oft displays
His thoughts of what she does and says,
And he is known, I believe, to shine
As a sagacious, learn'd divine.
He has free entrance at the Hall,
Whenever he is pleas'd to call,
Though I've been told it is but rare
He's known to pay his visits there,
For when she's in a certain whim
She strives to play some trick with him.
—He says he's sure she will not stray
From virtues's fair and open way,
Nor that she e'er will give offence
To the mind's purest innocence,
But she's as lightsome as a fairy
In pranks and whimsical vagary :
As a coquette she daily dances,
Then gratifies blue stocking fancies;
To-day, to deck her charms inclin'd,
To-morrow to enrich her mind :
Nay, 'mong the *Jacks*, the *Dicks*, the *Harries*,
'Twill not surprise him if she marries,

If she chuse one of science full,
Or one impenetrably dull,
Some great man for his sterling sense,
Or parson for his eloquence:
Nor would he wonder, if through life
She ne'er renew'd the name of wife.
And now, Sir, you may form a notion
Of Madame *Omicron's* promotion."

It must be own'd that all his news
To Syntax was of sovereign use,
To shape the plans he had in view,
Inform him what he had to do,
And how and in what way to woo.
—Thus arm'd, he sent Pat on before,
T' announce his coming at the door,
Where Madame O——, with smiling face,
And the most condescending grace,
Gave her best welcome to the cot,
Which was her philosophic lot,
For such she nam'd the charming spot.
The walls were festoon'd o'er with flowers,
Here winged boys and there the hours
Floated along in airy ease,
The surface of the lengthen'd frieze;
And all around he seem'd to see
Some well-dress'd Pagan Deity.
She plac'd him in a satin chair,
'Tween MERCURY and JUPITER,
And plac'd a stool with fruitage drest
On which his either foot to rest.
—Thus seated 'mid the Olympic folk,
Syntax began to scent a joke;
And, fitting their forms to his own,
Doubted if he should smile or frown.

Dʀ SYNTAX WITH A BLUE STOCKING BEAUTY

IN SEARCH OF A WIFE

"If this," he thought, "be classic fun,
I'll gravely wait what's to be done;
If of the scene I am the jest
I'll work my way and act my best."

    The Doctor felt that his queer phiz
Was such as might invite a quiz;
For, right or wrong, he seem'd to see
Quizzing was her propensity.
At all points therefore he prepar'd
To keep himself upon his guard,
In *jesting* to give joke for joke,
If it were *wit*, give stroke for stroke;
If learning he were call'd to ply,
To mix it up with flattery,
And cull from poets and from sages
The gallantries of former ages.

    An antique tripod now appear'd
Upon three grinning Satyrs rear'd,
And at each corner there was wrought
The visage of a bearded goat;
The basins which contain'd the tea
Show'd ornamental sympathy,
For they shone bright with golden darts,
The cakes too bore the form of hearts,
While the dark vase that held the cream
Did the Etruscan fabric seem.

    —And now a glove the Widow dropp'd,
When up in haste the Doctor popp'd,
To give back with an eager grace,
The fallen trifle to its place;
When the stool tripp'd, and threw him o'er
In sprawling length along the floor:
The tripod also sought the ground,
The goats and satyrs lay around,

And china's broken forms display'd
The ruin which his fall had made.
—Ma'am to the bell plied such a stroke
That the rich silken cordage broke,
And pale-fac'd maids came rushing in
To know what caus'd the mighty din.
The Doctor rose, confus'd, amaz'd,
And on the shatter'd ruins gaz'd,
When he exclaim'd, " The best design
Doth often meet a fate like mine ! "
But soon the sage was kindly greeted
And soft consoling words repeated.
" O be not at this bustle griev'd
If you no mischief have receiv'd,
If safe in hand, if safe in arm,
Let not your looks express alarm ;
O never, never mind the rest,
And be not, Doctor, so distrest !
Genius does awkward things they say—
I'm doing them, aye, ev'ry day :
And, when that you shall know me better,
You'll find in me, Sir, *à la lettre*,
What POPE so honours with applause,
That temper which, whate'er the cause,
Ne'er makes complaint, nor frowns, nor squalls,
E'en though the fav'rite china falls.
But to dispel your startled care,
In the next room we'll seek a chair,
And Bacchus' self shall meet you there."

" —A chair," said Syntax, " by your leave,
I will with your commands receive,
But, please you, I'll excuse the stool
Which caus'd me thus to play the fool,
Unless you can procure me one
To mourn the mischief I have done ;

Where I may seat me and repent,
In form of awkward penitent."
—The Dame exclaim'd, with uplift eye,
As if in rapt'rous extacy,
"O bravo, Doctor! O what a wit!
How nicely too you manage it!
All the best china I've in store
I'd willing see upon the floor;
O it would be a trifling price
To make the paltry sacrifice,
If but my fancy would take wing,
And make me say so good a thing!
But wit like yours is never taught,
Nor can with power of gold be bought;
'Tis genius, or the happiest nature,
That of this gift is the creator;
But she forgot as you may see,
To give th' awak'ning charm to me.
Hence 'twould be venial if from you
I could purloin a flash or two,
To keep for use and lively play,
Upon some chosen, gawdy day."

That quiet spirit call'd self love,
So apt the human breast to move,
Began a little place to find
Within the Doctor's wav'ring mind;
And, if it did not turn them out,
Was prone to calm each rising doubt;
While the warm sense of conscious pride
Inclin'd him to the flatt'ring side
Of what the smiling widow spoke,
Whether in earnest or in joke.

He now a sofa's corner grac'd,
On the same seat the Dame was plac'd,

Though to some distance she retir'd,
As chaste, decorous form requir'd.
In gilded frame there hung between,
From Titian's hand, a fav'rite scene,
Where young Adonis did appear ;—
A boar's head crown'd the pointed spear,
While 'neath the silken folds behind
The doting Venus lay reclin'd.
The lady cast her eyes above
As if she view'd the Queen of Love,
Then to her side a look she threw,
Where she had Syntax in her view ;
But it was rather to explore
The heads of Syntax and the boar,
When whim endeavour'd, if it could,
To find out some similitude,
While her gay fancy strove to rig
The beast's head in a parson's wig.
—Some little chit-chat 'bout the arts,
But not a word as yet of *Hearts*,
Of ling'ring time fill'd up the measure,
'Till supper waited Madam's pleasure,
Which was in tasteful order set
In an adjoining cabinet,
Whose classic paintings, like the rest,
The genius of the place confest.
—Two Bacchanalian infants lay
Upon a tiger's skin at play,
Beneath an overshadowing vine
Around the elm whose branches twine,
And purple clusters hang between
To give a richness to the scene ;
While views of wood and water-fall
Are scatter'd o'er the crimson wall :
But Syntax look'd to satisfy
His palate rather than his eye,

IN SEARCH OF A WIFE

And that eye was dispos'd to stare
When it beheld the bill of fare.

One dish a single pigeon grac'd,
On t'other side three larks were plac'd;
A tart, about two inches square,
Cut out and fashion'd like a star,
Potatoes two, most nicely roasted,
The produce which her garden boasted,
And in the midst, the eye to please,
A milk-white Lilliputian cheese,
Were all arrang'd in order due,
And look'd so pretty to the view.

The Doctor, who so long had fasted,
Nor since 'twas noon a morsel tasted,
Besides he had kick'd down his tea,
Beheld this festive symmetry
Deck'd out in all the simple cost
That Wedgewood's pottery could boast,
In hungry fury, almost able
With the scant meal to eat the table:
Nay, while the puny bits she carv'd,
Poor Syntax fear'd he should be starv'd.
The wine was call'd, the summons cheer'd
His spirits till the wine appear'd.
Two minniken decanters shone
Like twenty prisms form'd into one;
Nay, with such lustre did they shine,
The eye could scarce discern the wine,
And quite perplex'd his eager sight,
To know if it were red or white.
The Hostess fill'd her ready glass,
And did the health to Syntax pass:
It held what might just wet her lip,
But was not large enough to sip.

Then, with *Bon Soir!* her guest was greeted,
And he the sleepy toast repeated:
But the cheering hopes were o'er,
The gay decanters held no more.
" I'm tir'd with our sheep-shearing feast,"
She said, " and long for balmy rest.
Hence, Sir, you will excuse my dress,
As I've just been a shepherdess,
And therefore suited my array
To the employment of the day:
To-morrow I'll put on my best
In honour of my honour'd guest."
She order'd then her chamber light,
Wish'd calm repose and bade good night.

    The Doctor follow'd in high dudgeon,
At having been so tame a gudgeon;
Hungry and sore with discontent,
He growl'd and mutter'd as he went,
" Of starving jokes, I'll make her sick,
And faith I'll play her trick for trick,
Before to-morrow's course is run,
I will return her fun for fun:
And may my hopes all go to pot,
If my resentment is forgot!"

    Poor anxious Pat begg'd leave to know
What seem'd to plague his Rev'rence so:
Nor did his kind enquiries fail
Of hearing the droll, starving tale.
" 'Tis strange," he in his way replied,
" For I, Sir, thought I should have died,
Of roast and boil'd, of bak'd and fried:
Not such a kitchen one in twenty,
So cramm'd with overflowing plenty.

But just permit me to observe,
Your Rev'rence surely need not starve;
You may defy, though you've forgot,
The utmost spite of spit and pot;
For safe within your great-coat pocket,
As big as any two-pound rocket,
A fine Bologna is well-stow'd
By way of prog upon the road;
And many a biscuit too pack'd up,
On which your Rev'rence now may sup,
Nor do I think that I shall fail
To get a jug of foaming ale."
He said, and soon the ale appear'd,
The sight the Doctor's spirits cheer'd,
And to complete his well-laid plot,
A nice clean pipe he also got;
Nay more, some high-dried weed he brought,
Without which pipes are good for nought.
The sausage gave its poignant slice,
The biscuit too was very nice;
He gave a whiff, the ale he quaff'd,
And at the Widow's banquet laugh'd:
The feast, which mov'd his humble pride,
Now shook with mirth his aching side.
Thus with these means of consolation,
And cure of thought that brings vexation,
Syntax dismiss'd his faithful valet
To snore the night out on his pallet;
While in arm-chair, with half shut eye,
He spoke a brief soliloquy:

"Thou welcome tube, to whom belongs
To make the mind forget her wrongs,
Thou bid'st my keen resentment cease
And yield to harmony and peace!

The Widow's mischief now is o'er,
And I shall frown and fret no more,
But arm myself with watchful care,
To fall into no other snare:
Nay, if her genius should succeed,
I'll bid good humour meet the deed;
And let her frolic and her joke—
If she must have them—end in *Smoke*!"

At length he felt 'twas time to rest,
And Morpheus claim'd him as his guest,
When in due time, refesh'd and gay,
He hail'd the promise of the day,
And in the book-room was display'd
The luxury of breakfast laid.
His eyes now joyous wander'd o'er
The contrast of the night before:
The tea in fragrant fumes ascends,
The sister coffee too attends,
While many a smoking cake appears
In butter sous'd o'er head and ears;
Boil'd eggs, slic'd beef and dainty chicken
Invite him to more solid picking,
While honey of delicious taste,
Adds sweetness to the morn's repast
But Syntax here was all alone,
For Madam did not rise till noon;
So that there were no forms to tease him
And he could take whate'er might please him:
Nor did he the free choice refuse,
He pleas'd his taste, he read the news,
Then search'd the well-rang'd shelves, to find
A classic breakfast for his mind.
He now took Ovid and Lucretius
To con o'er what those poets teach us,'

IN SEARCH OF A WIFE

That if he should be left alone
With this same Madam Omicron,
He might th' important question move,
Of the Philosophy of Love;
And find, at least, how all things stood;
If with success she might be woo'd,
Or, as he thought, if he should be
A play-game to her vanity:
Though, if her fancy should not chuse him,
Her fine vagaries might amuse him,
At all events, he was prepar'd
To take what fortune should award.
The Dame, howe'er, he did not see
'Till the house-clock had sounded three.

   She now appear'd in all the pride
Of figure and of ton beside:
Her form was fine, for plastic Nature
Had work'd with pleasure on her stature.
Of those bright, heav'nly rivals three,
Who call'd on Paris to decree
The envied apple, form'd of gold,
The Dame seem'd cast in Juno's mould,
To whom 'tis by the poets given
To wear the breeches e'en in Heaven;
And Madam, as her neighbours sing,
Would do on earth the self-same thing.
Grand, full of animated grace,
The chasten'd smile play'd on her face,
And though old Time, that scurvy fellow,
Had brought her to be more than mellow;
Yet taste and art contriv'd to shade
The inroads which his hand had made.
The Doctor view'd her to and fro;
And eyed her form from top to toe,

Transfix'd he stood by wild surprize
Told by his tongue and by his eyes,
And stammer'd, for he scarce could speak,
A line in Latin, then in Greek:
Nay told her that she rivall'd Eve,
Who did from Milton's strains receive
That praise which dwells on every tongue,
And has by many a Muse been sung.
The thought with flatt'ring brilliance shone,
And more than pleas'd Ma'am Omicron:
For though each self-prevailing thought
Was with a lurking laughter fraught,
Yet her heart aim'd not at concealing
A pleasure at the Doctor's feeling;
Who, from his lips as well as eye,
Gave fuel to her vanity.
Her thanks with so much grace were given,
That Syntax seem'd half-way to Heaven;
Nay, his heart beat with such delight,
He fancied he had got there quite.
She now propos'd a garden walk
Where, in some sentimental talk,
They might the sun-shine hours consume,
'Till summon'd to the eating-room.
"—O plaintive Hammond, how he shines,"
Said Syntax, "in these charming lines!

' How sweet to wind along the cool retreat
 To look and gaze on Delia as I go;
To mingle sweet discourse with kisses sweet
 And teach my lovely scholar all I know!' "

She bow'd, and with a side-long glance,
Threw the poor Doctor in a trance,
In which he felt strong inclination
To hint at Love's o'ercoming passion;

But still he felt afraid to stir,
'Till he receiv'd a hint from her.

  They gain'd the slope, they sought the glade,
Or, seated 'neath the beechen shade,
They search'd those principles of taste,
Which to Elysium turn the waste;
Here make the crystal waters flow,
Or dash from heights on rocks below,
And there erect the portico;
Or column raise, or sink the grot,
But ne'er let nature be forgot.
Through fragrant shrubberies they rove,
But not a word was said of Love,
'Till they approach a basin's side,
In whose transparent waters glide
The fish, who their bright forms display'd
In gold and silver scales array'd.
"I do not as Narcissus did,
Of whom in classic tale we read,"
Syntax exclaim'd, with fond delight,
"I view not in the mirror bright
My meagre self; a form divine
Does in the liquid crystal shine.
Ah, Lady, and I feel it true,
The shadow steals its charms from you!
Here would it stay when you were gone,
And thus be seen when you are flown,
Here would I ask a cot, and gaze
Through the bless'd remnant of my days."
But on the vision too intent,
O'er the green brink he fondly bent,
And sudden dash'd into the water,
While Ma'am ran off to hide her laughter,
And send her household to await
The Doctor in his dripping state:

But the mirror was so shallow
There was not room to sink or wallow;
And without aid he soon was seen
Shaking his wet legs on the green:
But Pat his ready help applied,
And soon each moisten'd part was dried.

The dinner was a plenteous feast
Where ev'ry varying dish was best,
And Bacchus in the realms above
Ne'er furnish'd better wine for Jove.
Thus when he had his fill of both
And all was mov'd off with the cloth,
Thought Syntax, "I'm not such a fool
To let a dip my courage cool;
Besides, with Heaven's own vintage warm'd,
I feel that I am doubly arm'd,
And will not any longer wait,
To try my chance and know my fate."
But while he his best looks prepar'd
To see what fortune might award,
He was address'd in gentle tone,
And ask'd by Mrs. Omicron,
If by his logic he could prove
Where was the real seat of Love;
She begg'd that philosophic spirit,
Which Fame allow'd him to inherit,
To fix and settle her opinion
As to its rights and its dominion.
—This was the topic which he sought,
And such the doctrine which he taught.
"—*Lucretius*, now before me, says
(A poet whom all lovers praise)
That love is seated in the liver,
That there the Boy exhausts his quiver;

While *Ovid* sings it is the heart
In which he aims to dip his dart:
For me I know not how to trace it,
Unless 'tis where you chuse to place it."
"—Pooh! Pooh!" she said, "I'm grown so stupid,
As to forget the laws of Cupid;
Nay, having lov'd a husband once,
I am become so great a dunce,
That now I think 'twould be in vain,
Howe'er I strove—to love again."
"Nonsense!" th' enliven'd sage replied,
"Take my experience for your guide:
No greater weakness than to mourn
And weep beside a husband's urn:
Believe me 'tis an idle whim,
When you've your duty done to him,
Not such an useless grief to smother
And do that duty to another.
Still, while the form of beauty lives,
And the cheeks' roseate glow survives:
While sympathetic feelings warm,
And hope and fear may wake alarm,
It is the sober call of reason
To cull the fruitage of the season,
To love again, again to coo,
And wed—as you and I might do."

 He paus'd—a willing ear he lent
To hear his hope's accomplishment,
But Ma'am said *nought*—though that's *consent*,
He thought, if but the adage old
Does a decided truth unfold;
At least he chose thus to infer
And be self-love's interpreter:
Though soon this charm the lady broke,
And thus with serious aspect spoke.

"The dream in which your fancies shine
Will never be a dream of mine,
No ne'er again my heart will prove
The pleasures or the pains of love;
Whether 'tis in the heart or liver,
I defy Cupid and his quiver,
Though I may not disdain the hour
Which bears me into Hymen's bower,
But then it will be reason's care
To lead me as a votary there;
And all that I shall look to find
Will be the husband of my mind.
Or be he fat, or be he thin,
Whether his long and pointed chin
Appears as if it meant to rest
Upon the cushion of his chest,
Or if his prolongated nose
Should guard his grinning mouth from blows,
Whether the one or t'other eye
Or both indeed should look awry.
I care not—'tis his sense refin'd,
And chaste decorums of the mind,
Which will my inclinations move
To join in pure seraphic love."

The Doctor wonder'd at the whim,
But it might be a hint to him;
So, on his steady purpose bent,
He still pursued his argument.
—He reason'd long, he reason'd deep,
He reason'd 'till she fell asleep:
He saw indeed her eyes were clos'd,
Though he ne'er fancied that she dos'd,
But thought she took this blindfold course
To give attention greater force.

The tea and rattling china's sound,
Now 'woke her from her sleep profound;
But 'twas again to hear him prove,
What ancient bards had sung of love,
And what philosophers had wrote,
He did not fail with warmth to quote:
The subject was not of her chusing,
But still she found the sage amusing:
Science and wit he did combine,
'Till the turret-clock struck nine,
When there appear'd the ev'ning wine,
With season'd sandwiches to boot,
That would the nicest palate suit.
—To the Muse it is not known
Whether it were from frolic done,
The Doctor's high-flown thoughts to quicken,
And cause the evening plot to thicken,
But the round tray did not resort
To the dull flow of humble port,
Inspiring champagne, sparkling, bright,
Was the rich order of the night,
When Syntax, having whet his whistle,
Seiz'd on the high-wrought, fam'd epistle
Which *Sappho* to her *Phaon* wrote;
A poem far too long to quote,
But, mov'd by the impassion'd verse
That did the lover's pains rehearse,
Or whether the enliv'ning juice
Had made his spirits too profuse,
The widow felt the gay divine
Dispos'd to act the libertine;
And therefore thought it time to rule
His wilfulness to play the fool.

"Doctor, you just now talk'd of livers,
Of bleeding hearts and Cupid's quivers;

But you would wish me to suppose
Love makes his entry at the toes,
Or wherefore do you thus incline
To let your broad foot press on mine.
For shame, Sir, you who court the Graces!
Your feet are in improper places;
Why, my good friend, it is most shocking,
You'll rub the blue, Sir, off my stocking.
Susan, I'm sure, will look askew,
If on the clocks she chance to view
The symptoms of your awkward shoe."
Instant she rose and seiz'd the light,
" 'Tis time," she said, "to say good-night."
"Good-night," in rapture he repeated,
And thus his hurrying hostess greeted.
"But ere you go, O let me sip
Th' ambrosial sweetness of your lip!"
One warm salute he stole—no more,
Though he attempted half a score:
But she her open hands applied
To his lank cheeks on either side,
Then gave his ears a wringing pull,
Twitch'd his long nose, and rapp'd his scull,
Turn'd his fine wig all o'er and o'er,
And brought the hinder part before;
Blew out the light, and off she went,
As if on bitter vengeance bent.

"Susan," she said, "my rev'rend spark
Is left completely in the dark:
So get a light, that he may clamber
With all attention to his chamber;
Then give him to his servant's care,
That he may do no mischief there."
Susan obey'd, but scream'd to see
Such an alarming effigy,

When the recover'd Syntax said,
"Tell me, I pray, my pretty maid,
With what your mistress is possest
That thus she treats her rev'rend guest."
"Lord Sir, believe me, 'tis no more
Than she has often done before;
One of my lady's lively airs,
For she's gone laughing up the stairs
To her own room—to say her pray'rs."
"Well," he then thought, "I will refrain
From sense of wrong, nor e'er complain:
She will not, I now think, expose
My suff'rings from her doughty blows,
And as she laughs, I will not cry;
She'll keep the secret—so will I."

He now approach'd his welcome bed,
But ere he laid his aching head,
Pat was inform'd, at early hour
He should proceed upon his Tour.
But yet he did not like to go
Without returning blow for blow,
Not as a fretful, angry stroke,
But half in earnest, half in joke;
And thought he could not do it better,
Than by an unexpected letter.
His was a short, disturb'd repose,
When from a silken bed he rose,
Just with the sun;—he then began,
And thus the sly epistle ran:—

M<small>ADAM</small>,
With all regard that's due
I offer these few hints to you;
The best return that I can make,
And which you will in kindness take,

*For all your laughing, quizzing, eating,
Not to forget the precious beating
Which, such was your correcting zeal,
As I now write I still can feel.*

*Last night, I know, I play'd the fool,
And serv'd to wake your ridicule:
Your wit, your wine, your gay pretences,
Must have depriv'd me of my senses,
Or surely, I should ne'er have done
What I now blush to think upon.
Could I suppose, when I came here,
That one like me had aught to fear?
Say, could I think of aught so shocking
As Mock'ry clad in* azure stocking?
*The Muses and the Graces too
I thought to find in* garter blue,
*That which old proverbs do maintain,
Is never known to bear a stain.
And, with my sable rev'rend hue,
The chasten'd fancy might review
A union rare of* BLACK *and* BLUE.
*I hop'd to list beneath the banners
Of high-wrought mind and graceful manners,
All which, enliven'd I should see
With philosophic pleasantry,
While hearts congenial might consent
To join in tend'rest sentiment.
—Such were my hopes, nor need I tell
What fortune those same hopes befell.
Fine taste and elegance I own
I look'd for in* MA'AM OMICRON,
*And they I know might suited be
To deck, as I had hop'd to see,
The most refin'd simplicity.*

But lo! there enter'd in its stead,
What you'll remember, while you read,
Well manag'd trick and ready laughter,
Nor will I tell what follow'd after—
For I can only take for granted,
That, by some art, I was enchanted.
—And now, as I am taking leave,
Deign my kind counsel to receive.
You laugh at others, and what then?
They may return the laugh again.
How ready's your sarcastic word,
With She's a fright, and He's absurd!
But while at others' faults you frown,
Think you, alas, that you have none?
'Tis time, if I have eyes to see,
To quit your frisky mockery,
In five years you'll be Forty-three!
That secret I've contriv'd to trace,
Besides the dial on your face,
Believe me, Madam, tells as true
As any household clock can do.
Youth may be pardon'd when it plies
Its soft or sprightly coquetries,
And even be allow'd to bear
The flattery which courts its ear.
Indeed, I'm not so idly bold,
As e'en to hint that you are old,
Yet I can ne'er allow my tongue
To err, in saying you are young.
Your beauty, though once overflowing,
Is like an auction lot—a-going:
In vain, Ma'am, you may scold and frown,
Time's hammer soon will knock it down,
And I do not forbode a stir
Of who will be the purchaser.

Why, think you, that I could not see,
Midst all my words' embroidery,
You wear a Wig—as well as me?
Nay, I could name a striking feature
That's deck'd by art and not by nature,
Though such your taste, I do confess,
When, in the splendid show of dress,
So well trick'd up your form appears,
You lose full half a dozen years.
But yet I own the radiant eye,
Which still may wake th' admiring sigh;
Whose stern look still may cause alarm,
And whose soft, smiling beam may charm,
Nay, I with warm assent allow,
While I with ready homage bow,
That you possess the mental grace,
That in your character I trace
A mind with ample powers endued,
To please the learned and the good.
Let then your affectations cease,
Give joy, do good, and live in peace.
—Quit then, O quit your CIRCE's *Art,*
By which you play a treach'rous part!
O leave the witch'ry of her school,
Nor turn a wise man to a fool!
Strive from all whims your mind to free,
And think not, you e'er laugh'd at me.
—Thus I present my farewell warning,
And to your night-cap bid GOOD-MORNING.
With all regard your virtues claim,
I humbly sign my humbled name,
      SYNTAX.

Thus as he did the letter fold,
"I may," he thought, "have been too bold,

But have I not been as severe
On my own folly as on her?
If I can check these wayward tricks,
And her fine understanding fix,
(Fond Nature's gift improv'd by art)
And give right impulse to her heart;—
If I can damp her lively glory,
In chanting forth my silly story,
To make the grave Blue Stockings laugh,
While they their evening beverage quaff,
And that their meeting may be jolly,
By heighten'd pictures of my folly,
This letter, thus well understood,
May prove the source of real good."

Now with a sort of doubtful whistle
He wafer'd close his warm epistle,
And without pause, he thought it best
To leave the letter thus address'd:

"*This packet Susan's bid to take,
When Madam chuses to awake.*"

This done he did no longer wait,
Punch ready stood;—he mounted straight,
And trotted briskly through the gate.

CANTO XXXVI

Now Syntax was, it might be thought,
To serious contemplation wrought
By all he had so lately seen,
Nay what he had so lately been,
That there was matter to supply
Twelve miles of good soliloquy.
But he wish'd not his mind to fix
On the strange widow and her tricks:
For though, as he employ'd the key,
T' unlock the gates of memory,
Some motley whimsies might appear,
Which had found a sly corner there,
And would awake a sense of mirth;
Yet he must feel that they gave birth
To certain interludes beside,
Which serv'd to wound his solemn pride.
For, though so pure might be his aim,
Reflection gave him much to blame;
And 'stead of furnishing content,
Still conscience whisper'd him—*Repent.*
Thus in the struggle to forget
The being caught within the net,
Where nought that he had hop'd was gain'd,
Nor e'en the slightest good obtain'd;
Of all his usual life bereft,
He neither look'd to right nor left,
Nor down to earth, nor t'wards the spheres,
But onward 'tween his horse's ears,

Where to a point his eyes he brought,
Which, though wide open, yet saw nought;
A situation often known
To thought, when it is left alone.
At length the pensive Doctor dos'd,
And both his eyes were quickly clos'd;
For a soft, all-subduing sleep
Did on his senses gently creep,
And PAT, a faithful servant he,
Did on this sleepy point agree.

    This page attempts not to explore,
As *Æsop* did in days of yore,
How beasts and birds and reptiles thought,
And by what potency were taught
To think and speak and act like men,
Which they don't now—if they did then.
Monkeys, it seems, might grin and vapour,
There cut a joke, here cut a caper;
The lion might be call'd to rule,
An Elephant might keep a school:
The Snake, with gratitude at strife,
Might strike at his preserver's life;
While, from base, mean and selfish ends,
The hare might lose her many friends;
And thus the animals dispense
The sterling rules of common sense.
But well-fed *Punch* was form'd by nature
A mere instinctive, useful creature;
Who, on the road or in the stable,
Would not have answer'd for a fable:
Sure-footed, subject to no whim,
And sound alike in wind and limb;
Who both the whip and spur obey'd,
In the proportion they were laid;

But if he happen'd not to feel
An angry hint from thong or steel,
He, by degrees, would seldom fail
T' adopt the gallop of a snail.
Just now, then it may be suppos'd,
That, while his drowsy rider dos'd,
He thought he had a right to go
As slow as any horse could do:
But still he chang'd his forward way
To ease a passing cart of hay,
Or to the right or left would pass
To snatch a tempting tuft of grass.
The sun grew hot and *Punch* was dry,
A rippling brook was running by:
Towards the clear stream his way he bent,
Snuff'd the cool air, and in he went;
When, after having drunk his fill,
His feet were cool'd and he stood still;
And, feeling neither whip nor spur,
He thought there was no hint to stir.
PAT did the self-same footsteps trace,
And his horse sought the self-same place.
Thus, side by side, the cattle stood
Knee-deep within the crystal flood;
While fast asleep the riders sat,
The Doctor here, and there was Pat;
And how long on the river's lap
They might have thus enjoy'd their nap
It is not worth the while to guess,
It would of course be more or less;
But a rough tinker on his ass,
Happ'ning that morn that way to pass
Could not but think it rather droll
To see them sleeping cheek by jowl;
Nor could he check his rude, gruff laughter,
To hear them snoring o'er the water:

IN SEARCH OF A WIFE

Then, with a piece of solid metal
He struck with force a hollow kettle,
And instant the resounding stroke
The master and his valet woke.
With the sudden noise they started
And from their wat'ry station parted.
The Doctor thought a shot was fir'd,
And from what quarter he enquir'd;
The Tinker said, "You need not fear,
No enemy, good Sir, is here:
I travel all the country round,
To fill up holes, where holes abound.
I am a trav'lling, tink'ring stranger,
Who thought, Sir, that you were in danger;
For had you met an overthrow
In the mill-dam that is below,
'Twould have been labour all in vain,
To get your Honour out again:
And as I could not reach to shake you,
I made the noise I did, to wake you."
"I thank you, friend," the Doctor said,
"Kindness like yours should be repaid;
It is a debt, I freely own,
So, Patrick, give him half-a-crown."
Poor, tink'ring Tom was quite delighted,
Who look'd not to be thus requited,
For all he did and all he spoke
Was in the way of saucy joke:
But so it was, and off he went,
Singing his way, with loud content;—
While his brass kettles told the tale,
As they resounded through the vale.

"How long," says Pat, "we might have stay'd
In the quick waters' running shade,

And why my brown horse and your mare
Chose to take a position there,
Now I'm awaken'd, makes me stare:
For howsoe'er we slept or dos'd,
An' please you, Sir, our eyes were clos'd."
"Pat," said the Doctor, "you're a fool;
The morn was hot, the river cool,
The beasts were early out and dry,
And drowsy too, as you and I,
For I throughout the night before,
Had not slept out a second hour.
—But let us on our journey haste,
The breakfast time advances fast,
And I've within a certain power
That tells it me besides the hour.
Nor must you, Pat, forget to rig
In its first honours my last wig,
Renew its curls, and thus restore
Its form to what it was before.
Its air canonic was beset
By that vain, whimsical coquet,
To whom I owe resentment yet;
Though, as a Christian, it were better
Both to forgive and to forget her."

Thus as he reason'd to and fro,
Not yet determin'd what to do,
He reach'd a pretty town, whose name
Does not possess historic fame,
But boasts an inn which Syntax blest
For morning meal and welcome rest.
The wig with all due skill repair'd,
The chin dismantled of its beard,
His whole exterior made as smart
As could be done by Patrick's art,

He set off, with design to call
Ere the sun set at *Tulip-Hall*,
And on the way his mind supply
With gen'ral terms of botany,
Call on his mem'ry to review
Whate'er he once of *Flora* knew;
Then add sweet, sentimental bloom,
A type of offerings yet to come,
And with such fragrant hope prepare
A welcome from the flowery Fair.

Thus as he thought a voice behind,
Which seem'd to load the passing wind,
Exclaim'd—" What, Doctor, is it you?
My eyes, I thank them, tell me true:
And pray accept my solemn greeting,
At such an unexpected meeting."
Syntax replied, "The same receive,
Which I to Doctor *Julep* give."
—It turn'd out that their journey lay,
For several miles, the self-same way,
When the Physician thus began
To tell his visit and its plan.
" CAPIAS, the Lawyer, whom you know,
Left business some few years ago:
In short he now has given up thinking
Of ought but eating and of drinking.
Nay once a fortnight 'tis at least,
That, after some redundant feast,
For me he in a hurry sends
As one among his oldest friends,
To ease his overloaded paunch
Of what remains of ham and haunch,
And to exert my utmost power
His weaken'd stomach to restore.

But soon, alas, too soon I think,
His food will be confin'd to drink,
When he must yield to his disease,
And I shall lose his gen'rous fees;
For I am not asham'd to tell
The Lawyer pays the Doctor well.
Forgot is his Attorney's trim,
His wary tricks are chang'd to whim.
In stuccoed eating-room he dines,
But takes his glass with all his *wines*,
And where, to vary his regale,
The cask pours forth the foaming ale;
For to his cellar he descends,
And 'neath its vault he treats his friends.
There the ever-moving glass
Quickens the hours as they pass,
While the tale, the joke, the song,
The bacchanalian feast prolong.
There of his vintage he's profuse,
And e'en if BACCHUS were to chuse,
Wherever he might chance to dine,
With CAPIAS he would take his wine.
O, how I wish you would attend,
This visit to my jovial friend!
To him, dear Sir, you're not a stranger,
Nor will your virtue be in danger!
He'll kindly put you at your ease,
With him you'll do just what you please:
Nay, 'twill amuse you thus to see
And hear the strange variety."

"You know I'm not so very nice,"
Said Syntax, "to pronounce it vice
When friends in mod'rate glasses join,
And cheer their hearts with gen'rous wine;

Social love appears the best
When seated at the friendly feast,
Nor can it wound a D. D.'s pride,
When I've an M. D. by my side.
I'll therefore join this pleasant frolic,
But, if I chance to get the cholic,
You must, my learned friend, agree,
To cure the pain without a fee."

This by the Doctors twain agreed,
Well-pleas'd they on their way proceed.
Capias with smiles his guests receives,
And a loud, hearty welcome gives;
Nor did he cease repeated greeting
Till dinner came—and then to eating.
Not a word passed but when he boasted
The ven'son to a turn was roasted;
And of the dishes, as they came,
He told their excellence and name.
The dinner o'er, with thanks to Heaven
For all the various bounties given,
The bacchanalian suite attend
And to the cellar they descend,
In the vaulted cave benighted,
'Till, by suspended lanthorns lighted,
The colour'd blaze dispers'd the gloom
Of the subterranean room.
—Syntax on all around him gaz'd,
The more he saw the more amaz'd:
Bottles on bottles seem'd to rise
In every form, of ev'ry size,
And casks of large and lesser shape,
Rich with the juice of ev'ry grape,
Were there in order due maintain'd
By thirst luxurious to be drain'd.

—Syntax now felt himself inclin'd
T' indulge the impulse of his mind;
But this was not a time for thinking
'Mid such a fearful threat of drinking.

He now took the appointed seat,
Suspicious of the liquid treat,
Resolv'd to keep his reason clear,
And watch what might be doing there.
—*Capias* exclaim'd, "This is the toast,
Which in this place must rule the roast,
And my good friends, I'm sure, will see
Its claim to fair priority:
I give the LAW—to that are owing
The means that set these currents flowing:
He loudly then pronounc'd the word,
And strait the ruby bumper pour'd:
The Doctors both the reason saw
Of his just pref'rence to the Law.
—*Capias* again fill'd up his glass.
"The second toast that I shall pass
Julep with pleasure will receive,
'Tis one that he himself would give:
Here's PHYSIC—call'd the eye of science,
Life's firmest friend and best reliance:
Without it boldly I declare
I should not now be sitting here,
Thanks to the learned Doctor there.
You both, I think, forebode the next,
Or as a toast, or as a text;
Though last, the highest in degree,
So now I give DIVINITY."

The flowing wine here found a pause;
Capias talk'd loudly on the laws;

Drawn by Rowlandson

IN SEARCH OF A WIFE

When *Julep*, without vain pretence,
But with a ready eloquence,
Display'd his scientific knowledge,
As a learn'd member of the College;
While Syntax thought it best would suit
His priestly office to be mute.
Nor did the Lawyer now appear
To wish the Doctor's thoughts to hear,
For then he happen'd to be thinking
'Twas time to take again to drinking.
"To what we've drunk, we all agree,
And now," he said, "I'll give all *three*,
LAW, PHYSIC and DIVINITY!
—All toasting hence, my friends, will cease,
And each may do as he shall please."

Syntax who sat serenely by,
Kept on his glass a wary eye,
While the physician and his host
Grew rivals as to drinking most;
When the good-humour of the day
Seem'd to be melting fast away.

"Let me," said *Julep*, "recommend,
Good *Capias*, as your real friend,
From this wild drinking to refrain,
Nor let me counsel you in vain.
From that vast paunch what ills betide you,
As big as any cask beside you!
For, if you thus go drinking on,
I e'en must tap that *Human Ton*."

—"Tap me? I then shall ne'er recover:
No," *Capias* said, "'twill soon be over
Life's stream will quickly run to waste,
For what's tapp'd here can never last:

From long experience I must own,
Belly or cask, 'twill soon be gone.
But hark, you ignoramus elf,
Feel your own paunch and—tap yourself!
And now I'll ask the grave Divine
Which is the biggest, yours or mine!"

—" You, like your brethren of the law,"
Cried *Julep*, "always find a flaw,
And, as you strive to patch it o'er,
Contrive to make as many more.
This history I have the power
To lengthen out at least an hour,
But 'twould be painful to rehearse,
So I will sing it in a verse.

> When the terrible law,
> Lays its horrible paw
> On a poor man he's sure to be undone;
> Nay, 'twill cause his undoing
> And e'en prove his ruin,
> Though as rich as the Lord Mayor of London."

"Your tricks," said *Capias*, "never cease
To humbug health into disease:
And thus you find the wealthy ninnies,
Who take your pills and give you guineas.
You know, old Galen, this is true,
And I can sing as well as you.

> —You Doctors ne'er fail
> Whatever we ail,
>   To talk us all o'er as you please;
> For whether you cure us,
> Or in church-yard immure us,
>   'Tis the same—you all pocket our fees!"

IN SEARCH OF A WIFE

Thus they drank and thus disputed,
Thus they argued and confuted;
Thus they sang or strove to sing,
It was much the self-same thing,
With some little stammering;
Then they slept and woke again,
'Till the stable-clock struck ten.

Syntax to escape was thinking
From this beastly scene of drinking,
When he would almost have preferr'd
A hog-trough with the grunting herd:
Nay, as he rather had a feeling
That sleep was o'er his senses stealing,
He thought it better to remove
To some sweet place of rest above;
When, as he turn'd his heavy head
He saw behind a supper spread,
Attended by a household dame,
Whom we shall now Rebecca name.
Thither he dragg'd his wooden chair,
And took a fix'd position there:
To Becky's hand he gave a squeeze,
And thus address'd her—"If you please,
I'll taste your tempting toasted cheese."
"No, Sir," she said, "here's better picking
Broil'd ham and a nice mushroom'd chicken,
So season'd I should not be willing
To swallow it for twenty shilling;
Though as a relish, I can boast
The making an anchovy toast:
And something's here with name uncivil,
For our cook christens it a Devil."
—"A Devil, in any shape, sweet maid
A Parson fears not," Syntax said;
"I'll make him minc'd-meat, 'tis my trade.

But while your sav'ry bits I'm eating
Tell me what means this vaulted meeting?
Whence comes the whim and what's the cause
That moves this agent of the laws
To play a part that seems high treason
Against the sov'reign law of reason?"
"Through summer months, it is his rule,"
Rebecca said, "because 'tis cool.—
For the first hour of their descent
'Tis all kind words and compliment,
But sure as my stool is a barrel,
They first dispute, and then they quarrel,
Then sleep and wake and snort and snore
'Till they, dear souls, can drink no more.
—It is my office to appear
With this superfluous supper here;
For, when before them I have plac'd it,
Heav'n bless the topers, they ne'er taste it;
And while they sleep, I leave the cats
To guard the dainties from the rats.
But that self-same fat doctor there
Plays a sly game, as I could swear:
For though he drinks and talks and sleeps,
Yet he a careful measure keeps;
For he contrives to save his head,
And walks off steadily to bed;—
While Mr. *Capias*, to his cost,
Drinks 'till his ev'ry sense is lost,
When all the household, while they bless him,
Bear him up-stairs and there undress him.
He wakes at morn with aching head,
And rumbling stomach over-fed,
When *Julep* seats him by his bed.
The pill, the purge, the powders follow,
Which he, alas, is doom'd to swallow:

Then, for a grumbling week, forsooth,
He does not use a grinding tooth:
For nought is on his table seen,
But sago, broths and medicine.
Indeed, whene'er his room I tread,
To ope the curtains of his bed,
I almost fear to find him dead.
—The Doctor having done his deed,
Is by the grunting patient feed,
Takes leave and darts off, like a rocket,
With five fresh guineas in his pocket."

Said Syntax, "'Tis a wretched sight,
So let your fair hand take a light,
And show me where to rest to-night;
For, without any formal warning,
I will be off to-morrow morning;
And leave, sweet maid, my pious prayer,
A tribute to your gracious care.
As soon as cocks begin to crow,
I hope to be prepar'd to go."
But though those birds their matins sung
Before his wak'ning bell had rung,
It had not struck the seventh hour
When he was jogging on his Tour.

Some smiles they pass'd, but not a word
The Doctor or his man preferr'd.
At length his Rev'rence wish'd that Pat
Should let loose his amusing chat
Of what he did and all he saw,
While they were with the man of law.
"—Whate'er," he said, "I look'd to see,
Was just, Sir, what it ought to be.

So kindly Mrs. Becky chatter'd,
And Oh, how Pat from Cork was flatter'd!
Of the good things I had the best;
And, faith Sir, I'm not now in jest:
For Mrs. Becky was so kind,
That she, perhaps, might have a mind
In my warm heart to make a stir
If I had been a widower;
For when I told her I was married,
O quite another face she carried.
And please, you, Sir, could it be shown
That my sweet person were my own,
I could work up a bargain well,
As, if you please, I hope to tell.
I think 'tis true or I mistake,
That Becky butters well her cake
She does whatever she may please,
And she not only keeps the keys,
But faith nor does she think it worse,
She handles the old lawyer's purse.
Besides whene'er he turns to clay,
And that she looks for ev'ry day,
'Twas whisper'd in my ear that she
Expects a good round legacy.
Thus, when his guzzling season's o'er,
She will ne'er go to service more,
But be a comely, wealthy wife,
And bless some honest man for life;
Nay, had I been from marriage free,
I might have been the happy he."

He paus'd.—The Doctor ever kind,
Who felt what pass'd in Patrick's mind,
With smiling glance, gave this reply:
"I do not wish just yet to die,

But when, please Heaven, my course is run,
And life's appointed work is done,
Patrick may find that Syntax knew
His worth, and could reward it too."
The honest fellow touch'd his hat:
"My heart now thanks you, Sir, for Pat."
He softly spoke, and breath'd a sigh,
Then drew his hand athwart his eye:
And if 'twere ask'd what he felt there;
It might be said, a grateful tear.

They journeyed on nor fast nor slow,
But much as other people do:
And, at an anti-dinner hour,
Syntax was seated in a bower,
For bower it was, though we must call
The blooming mansion, TULIP-HALL.
Fresh, balmy sweets were found to breathe
From blushing vase or pendant wreath,
While springing flowers of ev'ry dye
Enchanted the admiring eye.
Nor was this all, the landscape's pride
With the gay garden's beauty vied:
Wide spreading groves with lawns between,
In summer foliage, grac'd the scene,
And the glittering streamlets play'd
In eddies through the sunny glade,
While flocks were scatter'd o'er the dale
Where tall pines whisper in the gale,
And midway, in th' ethereal blue,
The spire divides the distant view.

As Syntax did the landscape trace
The widow'd mistress of the place
Appear'd with welcome in her face,

Which she confirm'd with cheering voice.
"To see you, Sir, I do rejoice,
Pleas'd too that you did not delay
Your coming here beyond to-day:
We want just such a man as you
To please and to instruct us too:
For I expect three charming neighbours
Who aid me in my floral labours:
But I this counsel must impart;—
Cast a broad buckler o'er your heart:
For 'tis my duty, though a stranger,
To warn you of a certain danger.
Thus you will, now, your mind prepare
Our lively, social joys to share;
While I to-morrow shall decree
To Flowers and to Philosophy.
But as the toilette now attends
To deck me out to meet my friends,
I leave you, Sir, till I am drest,
To do whate'er may suit you best."
Then from her breast-knot gay she took
A nosegay, and, with gracious look,
"This gift," she said, "I pray receive,
It is the sweetest I can give."
"Nay," he replied, "the gift I view,
Is sweeter, since it came from you—"
And thus the young acquaintance grew.
—The Doctor up the village walk'd
And with the gazing peasants talk'd,
When as a church rose in his view,
He thought there was a parson too;
So to the vicarage he hied
Where at the window he espied
A damsel full of joke and laughter,
Who prov'd to be the parson's daughter.

DR SYNTAX PRESENTING A FLORAL OFFERING

He with respectful look and mien,
Ask'd if her father could be seen,
When, with quick speech and sprightly eye,
The fair one hasten'd to reply,
"I'm sorry you to-day are come,
As my dear father is from home,
For he is gone to take his station
At the Archdeacon's visitation."—
"Will you then say, my pretty dear!
That Doctor Syntax has been here,
And if it is my lot to stay
At TULIP-HALL another day,
If I to-morrow should remain,
I hope, sweet maid, to call again:
In the mean time, I pray, receive,
'Tis all, I fear, I have to give,
These flowers, in whose form is shown
A native beauty like your own;
And may it, many a coming year,
In all its present glow appear!"
He did his fragrant gift present,
She revell'd in the charming scent,
And smil'd a grateful compliment.
—A matron who was on the watch,
From upper window in the thatch,
Thought it but proper to descend,
And give the warnings of a friend.
"I'm sister, Sir, to our Divine,
Nay that Miss is a niece of mine,
And much I wish to hint to you
What my good brother's self would do;
That you must your keen thoughts prepare
To guard against some hidden snare,
By which you may become the tool
Of lady Tulip's ridicule:

For she delights, at the expence
Of men of gravity and sense,
To make some saucy trick prevail,
And furnish out a merry tale,
In which her well-fed guests combine,
And scandal-mongers love to join;
As by example will appear
From the recital you shall hear.

"Last week, she had the art to move
A neighb'ring 'Squire to offer love,
And while upon his knees he swore
He lov'd as none e'er lov'd before,
She scream'd aloud, while 'tis as certain,
Three Misses, hid behind the curtain,
Did with their added clamours rouse
The various guardians of the house,
Who in the carpet did enfold him,
And all along the flooring roll'd him;
Then squatted on him, but no further,
As they might run the risque of murther.
Embrown'd with dust, all hot and panting,
Cursing the hour of his gallanting,
How he recover'd, no one knows,
But round the neighbourhood there goes,
Or true or false, a curious story,
Which I decline to lay before you:
But wheresoe'er the 'Squire can move,
He hears the tale of making love;
And all repeat the carpet brawl
That shook the floors of TULIP-HALL.
Now, should this strange, capricious dame
Attempt on you some idle game,
Let not, I beg, your patience leave you,
Be calm, come here, and we'll receive you."

The Doctor thus was well prepar'd
To keep himself upon his guard,
And when he reach'd the hall, he found
Th' assembled Misses ranged around,
In the full ton, and rather pretty,
With apt pretensions to be witty.
—The dinner came with taste prepar'd,
And Syntax its rare bounties shar'd:
In the dessert fresh garlands bloom,
Whose odours fill'd the ambient room;
And much he thought the coming hours
Would blossom with the world of flowers,
Their classes, orders, native dyes,
Their species and varieties,
Their leaves, trunk, stem, supports and root,
Their flow'ring, with their seed or fruit;—
He thought they would Linnæus quote,
And all Miss Wakefield speak by rote.[1]
But not a word was said of flowers,
No sweets were there, they dealt in sours,
For not a thought dismiss'd a sound
But some known name receiv'd a wound.
Among the grave, they nought could see
But symbols of hypocrisy,
While those whom merry fancy rules
Were noisy and outrageous fools;
The grave, the gay, the old and young,
Felt the full malice of their tongue:
And as for beauty, not a grace
Was own'd to smile about the place.
Tea came, nor did its cheering water
Check the malignant, smashing slaughter:
For still they told of ev'ry feud
That did disturb the neighbourhood:

---

[1] An elegant Introduction to the *Science of Botany*, by Miss Priscilla Wakefield.

The gossip's tale and envy's gall
Resounded in the blooming hall.
—The Sage benignant utter'd nought
But thus indulg'd the secret thought:
"Where all these fragrant flow'rets blow,
Rue, wormwood, nettles, ought to grow."

    At length the temple of perfume
Was quitted for the billiard-room.
Ladies command, he must obey,
So Syntax took a cue to play,
Tho' he did not the laugh approve,
As he propos'd to play for *Love*,
Or when the usual sum was nam'd,
For which these ladies always gam'd.
But, yet it seem'd as if he won,
Though when the pastime they had done,
He was inform'd, and to his cost,
The several parties he had lost,
As they were coolly counted o'er
By the tall Miss who kept the score.
Whate'er he fancied in their feats,
He could not say he thought them cheats,
So he put on a smiling face,
And paid his losings with a grace.
—The ev'ning rather calmly past,
When they all said, good-night, at last;
And the next morn, the breakfast o'er,
The whole a pleasing prospect wore;
When Ma'am proposed to show the glory
Of her renown'd Conservatory,
Where every plant and flower was found
That takes a root in British ground,
While many a native it could boast
Of distant clime and foreign coast:

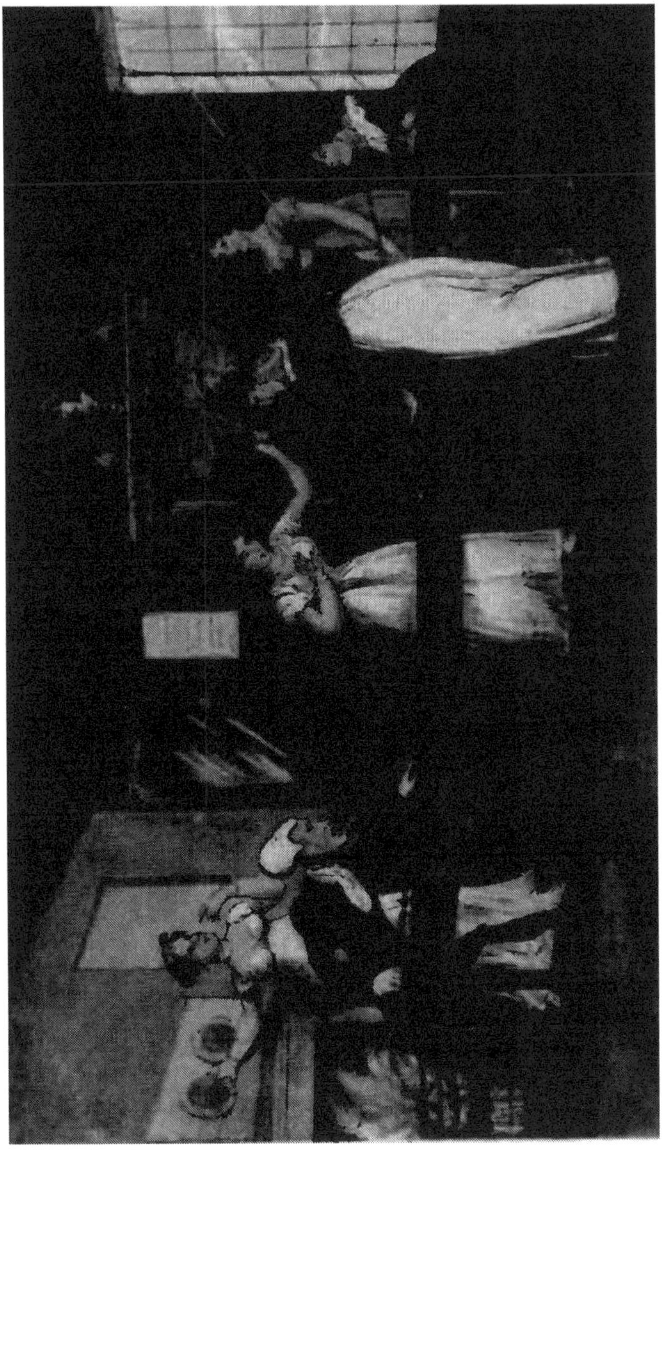

Nor did her fine harangue neglect
The true Botanic Dialect.
But just as Syntax felt inclin'd
To speak the impulse of his mind,
And, with a ready force, dispense
His scientific eloquence,
She urg'd him to direct an eye
To a fine Rose of Tartary:

"It is upon the upper row,
So mount, and bring it here below,
And I'll refresh it as I stand
With a full wat'ring-pot in hand."
Careful and step by step he mov'd,
But just as he successful prov'd,
A shelf gave way, another follow'd,
Ma'am Tulip scream'd, the gard'ner hallooed,
While Syntax join'd the gen'ral bawling,
And soon upon the ground was sprawling;
When, scatter'd round upon the green,
Pots, flowers and hat and wig were seen.
The lady trembling, from the spout
Let the cool, sprinkling water out,
Which did in various streamlets play
On Syntax as he struggling lay.
"O cease," he cried, "these rills to pour,
My head is neither pot nor flower,
And for the flowers my brains produce,
They're not for Lady Tulip's use:
If with these dripping favours crown'd,
Have mercy, or they'll all be drown'd."
He roll'd away and then uprose
His moisten'd drap'ry to compose;
But when she saw on looking round
The fragments scatter'd o'er the ground,

O never did the realms of Drury
Display a more decided fury.
"See," she exclaim'd, "you horrid *Bruin*,
The matchless mischief you've been doing!
These plants, I tell you, cost me more
Than a year's tithes could e'er restore.
Ill-luck in its worst guise, is seen,
In that beshrivell'd face and mien!
Be gone, you old, ill-boding fright,
Haste, leave my house, and quit my sight!
The lemon-scented moss that came
From——I've forgot the frightful name,
And my conundrum tulip's gone,
A flower so rare, that's scarcely known
In any hot-house but my own.
It makes my blood with vengeance boil,
That you this EDEN should despoil!"
"EDEN," he said, "it may appear,
For I behold a *Serpent* here;
Though not with one attractive feature
To tempt the heart of human creature."
"Gard'ners," she cried, "where are you all?
Expel this instant from the hall
This saucy parson, chase him hence,
And kick him for his insolence."
At him the wat'ring pot she threw,
His arms repell'd it as it flew,
When it return'd a hollow sound,
As it bounc'd from the verdant ground.
But when a fork she sought to wield,
The Doctor did not wait to yield,
But to the fury left the field;
And with quick steps the prudent Sage
Sought refuge at the Vicarage;
Where, with his pipe and balmy ale,
He jok'd and told his curious tale.

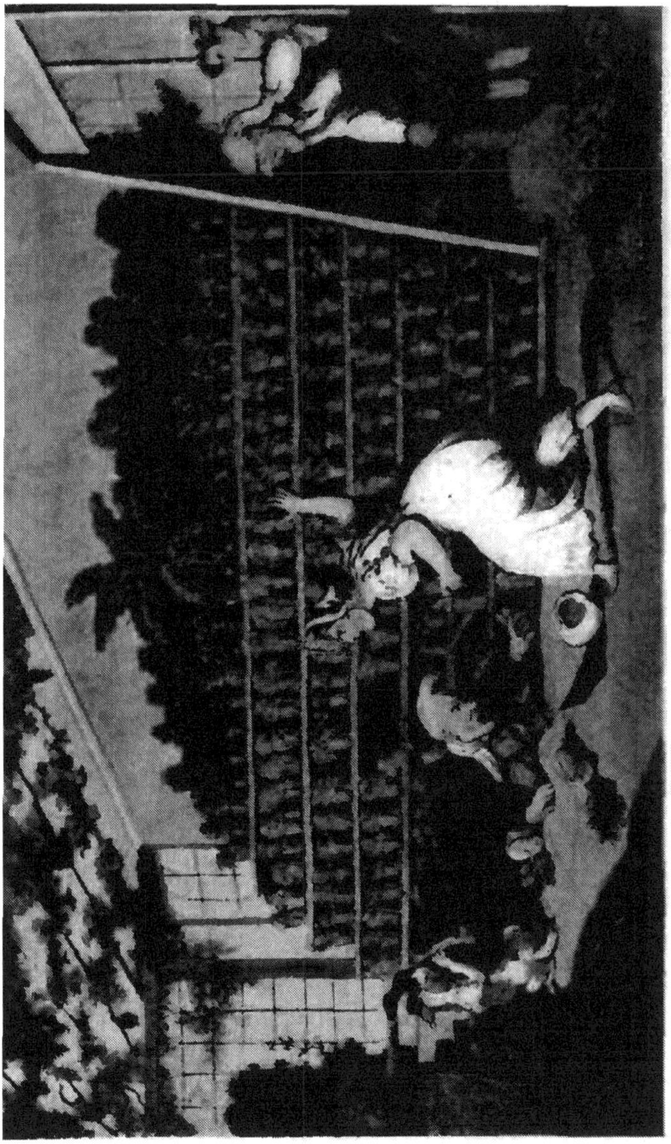

"But how," said he, "does she contrive
To keep this influence alive?
And what are they who thus submit
To her strange pranks and ribald wit?"
"Good Doctor Syntax, have you been
So many years in life's strange scene,"
The Vicar said, "and ask to prove
How all the various passions move?
Your experience sure can tell
Who know so much and think so well,
That, where the powers of wealth abound,
There humble parasites are found;
Whose base and reptile soul will bear
If they be said a soul to share,
The humbling tricks, and be the game
Of such a witch as Tulip's dame,
Brib'd by the feed she can afford
To offer at her plenteous board.
I hate her, as she loves to deal in
Pranks that betray such want of feeling.
Though wealth may this world's heaven impart,
That breast's a hell which wants a heart!
She strove one day to give me pain,
But she'll ne'er play that game again.
I let the haughty Madam see,
That a poor Vicar could be free,
And stamp upon her tyranny;
Nor do I think she's free from fear
Of him who is now sitting here.
She once seiz'd on my blushing daughter
To be a theme for open laughter,
But Sophy dear, who does inherit
A portion of her father's spirit,
Return'd a calm but modest dressing,
For which I gave the girl my blessing.

But as the Lady, from her store,
Is sometimes lavish to the poor,
Hence, as her due, respect attends,
Whene'er we meet—but there it ends."
Syntax his rev'rend host approv'd,
For 'twas the spirit which he lov'd.
—Thus having pass'd a cheerful day,
Tow'rds ev'ning he pursued his way.

As he jogg'd to his night's abode
The thoughtful trav'ller lost his road;
And as he stopp'd awhile to know
The ready way he ought to go,
The distant shouts of joy were heard,
But not a living soul appear'd.
At length Pat cried, "I see them come,
And 'faith, it is a harvest home."
Said Syntax, "What a charm to see
This show of glad simplicity!
How diff'rent this delightful scene
From those where we so late have been,
Where wealth dealt out its doles of folly,
Enough to make one melancholy."
The throng'd procession now drew near,
In front the mingled groupes appear
Of jovial peasants, who employ
Their voices loud, in hymns of joy.
Then comes the lab'ring waggon's load,
Dragg'd on along the winding road,
Rich with the sheaves the harvest yields,
The closing bounty of the fields.
—The Farmer, joy from top to toe,
With loud huzza led on the show,
While rustic music join'd the strain
Of HARVEST HOME, and cheer'd the plain.

IN SEARCH OF A WIFE

—Th' enliven'd Doctor thus addrest
The jolly master of the feast.
"My honest friend, I joy to see
This rich reward of industry,
And may this plenty still appear
To greet you many a future year,
And to your honest wish be given,
The bounties of indulgent Heaven!"
He then at once declar'd his name,
Told who he was, and whence he came,
And ask'd the farmer just to show
The way which he proposed to go.
"Leave, Sir," he said, "that thought behind,
It is an awkward way to find:
To-night, I pray, no further roam,
But stay, and join our Harvest Home;
And in the morn without delay,
I will conduct you on your way.
It will to us an honour be,
And by my looks I trust you see
I speak with humble honesty.
All welcome and respect that's due,
Shall, Rev'rend Sir, be paid to you:
Besides, Sir, and that's worth possessing,
Our feast will have your pious blessing.
O think not that the clam'rous noise
With which the peasant tells his joys,
Makes him forget to whom he owes
The plenty which the year bestows."
Said Syntax, "No!—It is the heart
That does the grateful sense impart:
Though rude the language, if the prayer
Can trace it to its fountain there,
Howe'er or whene'er it is given,
'Twill surely reach the courts of Heaven!

—Beneath the temple of the skies
You offer your glad sacrifice;
And that I join it you will see
From the example set by me."
—The dance, the music and the song,
United as they came along,
And gave a spirit to the scene,
Amid the gambols on the green.
—Syntax would now his skill display
Among the minstrels of the day,
And ask'd a fiddle to be sought;
The instrument was quickly brought;
It answer'd to his active hand,
When he march'd on and led the band.
The joyous show in rural state,
Now approach'd the mansion gate,
Where its delighted mistress stood
With comely look and smiling mood;
While her three daughters fair display
Their charms with flow'rs and ribbons gay,
And sung—" With joy we see you come,
Welcome, Welcome Harvest Home!"

The rural banquet now appear'd,
Each loaded dish was loudly cheer'd;
Beef roast and boil'd, the Briton's fare,
Was in abundant plenty there:
The pastry too, with walls of crust,
Waited the ploughman's eager thrust;
The pudding, with its plumbs well stor'd,
And many a cheesecake crown'd the board:
Nor was the custard, so renown'd
As rural dainty, absent found;
While *Bacchus* did to *Ceres* pay
The friendly homage of the day;

drawn by Rowlandson

THE HARVEST HOME.

Nor did his flowing tribute fail,
In copious jugs of foaming ale.
—The Sage uprose:—with solemn look
And silent preface, thus he spoke.

"To THEE, the giver of all good,
We offer up our gratitude,
For all the blessings that we share
From thy benign, paternal care;
And while our thanks we thus employ
For blessings which we now enjoy,
The crying wants of those supply,
Who bend beneath adversity:
Relieve them from thy plenteous store,
That they like us may want no more.
As Ravens from thy hand are fed,
O give us all our DAILY BREAD!
And in what state soe'er we move,
That all our doings may improve
Assist us, Gracious Power, and we
Shall learn thy laws—and live to THEE!"
—A chorus of Amens succeed,
Which gave the sign from word to deed.

The Doctor now resum'd his seat,
And smiling view'd the piles of meat;
When hasty hunger seem'd to wait
Round ev'ry dish, on ev'ry plate:
E'en sixty mouths were soon seen wagging,
And not a single jaw-bone lagging.
Ere a short hour was gone and past,
This mighty meal had seen its last,
While many an empty dish display'd
The change by hunger labour-made.
The brimming cups now took their round,
When jests and merry tales abound:

And social fun and many a joke
Blend with the pipe's ascending smoke.
The toasts are given, and jovial song
Does the gay, festive hour prolong.
Then to the garden turf they sped;—
The moon shone brightly over head,
And many a maid and many a swain
Tripp'd nimbly on the shaven plain;
Nor was their merry-making done
'Till Luna yielded to the Sun.
But just as Phœbus 'gan to peep
From his night's lodging in the deep,
The farmer thus his friends address'd:
"I give, ere we depart to rest,
The health of our kind, rev'rend guest,
With hearty thanks that he should come
To grace our humble Harvest Home.
The toast which I with pleasure give,
You will, with gen'ral joy receive;
Then join the heart-felt wish with me;
So here's his health—with THREE TIMES THREE!"

The Doctor felt an honest pride,
Then wav'd his hand and thus replied:—
"Think not because I preach on Sundays,
I may not aid your joy on Mondays!
Think not I fear dread Heaven's displeasure,
Because I guide your festive measure,
Or that I thus your feast prolong
With social mirth or lively song;
These doth indulgent Heaven dispense
To labour and to innocence.
—Continue worthy to receive
The bounties Heaven is pleas'd to give;
The blossoms of the fragrant Spring,
The Summer, when the valleys sing

With yellow harvest, and demand
The sickle in the reaper's hand:
The Autumn, when the fruitage glows,
Bending to earth the laden boughs;
And when the barn in Winter pours,
To pay your toil, its hoarded stores:
For these your hearts and voices raise
In humble prayer and grateful praise;—
And, in your various stations, move
With virtue, harmony and love.
Your duty crown with cheerful labour,
And upright dealings with your neighbour,
What conscience tells must not be done,
That is the deed which you must shun;
What conscience tells that you should do,
That is the way you must pursue;
And acting thus, you will possess
The surest means of happiness.
With patience bear the ills that wait
On mortal man, whate'er his state,
In lowly cot, or rich or great:
And when fair fortune beams its ray,
Grateful enjoy the prosp'rous day;
Whether 'tis sunshine or the storm,
To your known duties still conform.
Practise these lessons of a friend;
Then comfort will your lives attend,
And peace will bless your latter end."
—Thus did the Sage his counsels close,
Then sought his pillow's calm repose.

The Muse may have forgot the hour
When Morpheus yielded up his power,
And Syntax from his slumbers broke,
As if 'twere said—when he awoke:

And surely 'tis enough to say,
He found his spirits light and gay;
When, in their full and lively flow,
He join'd the worthy folk below;
Nor was the Don displeas'd to see
The morning's hospitality;
And to improve the plenteous fare,
The welcome smile abounded there.
—To all the Doctor's friends 'tis known,
And he himself will frankly own,
That whether good or ill o'ertakes him,
An active stomach ne'er forsakes him;
And he did such a breakfast make
On new bak'd loaf and oven-cake,
That they all look'd with wond'ring eye,
At his gaunt mouth's artillery.
—The *Honest Farmer*, such was known
His name and all his life to crown,
For 'twas in gen'ral use become
To call *Tom Truman* HONEST TOM,
Now hop'd his rev'rend guest would stay
And glad his house another day,
For still it would be holiday:
But Syntax said he must be gone,
And begg'd the favour to be shown
To *Crotchet Lodge*, the nearest way,
As there his promis'd errand lay.
"O," said the farmer, "from my grounds
You may see clear the wood that bounds
The place where Madam doth reside,
'Tis not a hasty hour's ride;
Within that time, I'm sure your mare,
With all her fat, will take you there."
—A smile now play'd on *Truman's* face,
On which the Sage thought he could trace

A certain inward, secret feeling,
That his good host aim'd at concealing;
Which, could he urge him to declare,
Might give him hints that would prepare
His mind with caution due to greet
Whate'er reception he should meet.
"Tell me," he said, "friend, what you know
Of this same place where I'm to go;
As it may be of use to me,
To hear what I perchance may see:
You would oblige me to explain
What whimsies haunt Miss *Crotchet's* brain,
As ladies who thus live alone
Are sometimes to odd habits prone,
And more so, when old maidens grown:
As, 'gainst her droll'ries should she show them,
I can protect me, did I know them;
Nor can you fear I should betray
What to my ear you may convey."
But while the farmer seem'd to doubt
If he should let the matter out;
The mistress of the mansion said,
"Why, Thomas, need you be afraid?
She's music-mad, the country knows it,
And ev'ry day her fancy shows it.
Where is a lady ever seen
To play upon a violin?
And more than half her time is spent
In scraping on that instrument;
And we have heard, when thus engag'd,
She looks a bedlamite enrag'd.
Sometimes she smiles and then will frown,
Casts her eyes up and then looks down,
Is known to swear as well as sigh,
And scream aloud in extasy;

Nay, she is even said to swoon,
When German Peg plays out of tune:
For while she works her fara-diddle,
The old girl strums a monstrous fiddle,
Of such a size, our Clerk can prove,
That asks a strong man's strength to move;
He as a workman did attend it,
And once was call'd in haste to mend it:
He says its belly would contain
More than will fill a sack with grain.
—Nor is this all, no not by half,
And oft her whimsies make me laugh.
When any of the straggling poor,
Relief to ask approach her door,
She does not question their distress,
Or how their wants she may redress,
But for an instant song will call,
And if they sing, whate'er their squall,
They're usher'd to the servants'-hall,
And 'mid the men and maids and boys,
She laughs and listens to their noise;
And those who chaunt a pleasant ballad,
Will to their roast meat get a sallad:
But if they cannot sing or play,
They pennyless are sent away.
Such are her whims, and many more
The country rumours have in store.
But when her music quits its tether,
Which sometimes haps for days together,
She then like other folks is seen
In quiet chat with easy mien.
—While thus postpon'd her music's labours
She hospitably treats her neighbours;
And then, perhaps, as you may see,
Madam is no more mad than me."

IN SEARCH OF A WIFE

The Doctor thus the matron heard,
And felt her story had prepar'd
His fancy to play off its art,
Not with a view to guard his heart,
For he no reason had to fear
That Crotchet's female chanticleer
Would e'er excite one idle wish
To dip in matrimonial dish.
He thought, with widows I have fail'd,
And now a maid must be assail'd:
I little from the scheme expect,
But still I'll not the chance neglect;
For this world's plans so strangely vary,
That oft our fairest hopes miscarry,
While sometimes those designs succeed
When dark despair beclouds the deed.
How oft when storms disturb the morn,
The sun's bright rays the moon adorn;
Nay, when the day has boist'rous been,
The evening's gay with smile serene.
Thus without much of hope or fear,
To *Crotchet-Lodge* my course I steer,
While I a cautious mind prepare
For all that may befall me there;
Ready to meet with steady eye,
Whether the fair-one may supply
Her DISCORD or her HARMONY:
E'en though she's govern'd by the moon,
She'll beat in time and scold in tune.
—And now, good friends, my thanks receive;
I wish that I had more to give!
But still my grateful thoughts are bent
On more than bare acknowledgment.
Permit me then, to say again
That my warm home is Sommerden:

Nay, what I mean, full well you know,
When, honest Tom, I tell you so;
And while I take you by the hand
My heart's regard you may command."
—Syntax now gave the dame a kiss,
As well as to each rustic miss
Who did the busy needle ply,
The boast of *Truman's* family.
Thus did he his farewell conclude
With the fond blessing of the good;
And soon his ready way pursued.

Of the gay Lodge he came in view,
And pac'd down the long avenue;
Where cages hung on ev'ry tree,
From which was heard the melody
Of birds, who in their nature rove,
The choristers of every grove;
But thus confin'd, the whole day long
They charm with their untutor'd song;
While fountains with their tinkling falls
Fill'd up the silent intervals.
The doors no noisy knocker plied
To bid the portals open wide;
But when the fingers touch'd the string
Soft silver bells in cadence ring,
Which a smart, tuneful Indian call
To give admittance to the hall,
While his big pouting lips dispense
The pipe's Pandean eloquence.
Thus Syntax did an entrance gain,
And soon his ear was charm'd to pain;
For, in each window there reclin'd
A harp that felt the sweep refin'd
Of the soft zephyrs' waving wind;

No hands could touch the strings so fine.
What sweet, what solemn airs divine
Now up the diapason roll,
Then sink again into the soul,
And wake sweet musings in the heart,
As seraphs did a hymn impart
Beyond the reach of mortal art;
And did enchantment soft supply,
By its aërial minstrelsy.

   The Doctor pass'd through many a door;
The little Negro walk'd before,
And, in his way, he play'd a tune,
'Till they had reach'd a gay saloon,
Whose ceiling and its walls display'd
A various kind of serenade,
Where all the Muses nine appear
In Heliconian character:
Nay, Music all around inspires;—
The very chairs are deck'd with lyres,
While satyrs, with their piping reed,
Support the sofa's lolling bed;
And clocks with spreading symbols screen
Their dials that they scarce are seen;
Not plac'd so much to mark the time,
As to play tunes and ring a chime.
The organ too, whose sound obeys
The nimble hand that sweeps the keys,
Or that whose settled tunes he finds
Whoe'er the turning barrel grinds:
And still the zephyrs breath'd the swell
Of sounds from power invisible.
—Thus the Doctor's ears and eyes
Were quite suspended with surprise;
In short, all that he saw around him
Serv'd to delight and to confound him.

He thought, if e'er beneath that roof
The harmonious virtues stood aloof,
Nay he was sure if Discord e'er
Should make a moment's entrance there,
The witch would vanish in despair.

Thus as his wav'ring mind compar'd
What he now saw with what he'd heard,
His faith began to be at strife
With the tale told by *Truman's* wife;
Nay other items did conspire
To set the old woman down a liar.
When, as he thus pursued his thought,
With grace and as a lady ought
Miss Crotchet enter'd, brisk and gay,
Apologis'd for her delay,
With pleasing smile possess'd a chair,
And welcom'd Doctor Syntax there;
Then did a slight discourse pursue
As other well-bred ladies do;
The weather and the road he came,
What news was on the wings of fame,
And if his neighb'ring Lakes had reason
To hope an overflowing season.
Thus she a sprightly turn display'd,
But not a word of Music said:
The Doctor, therefore, thought that he
Must enter upon harmony,
And what he saw and heard supplied
A theme to please the lady's pride.
Please her it did, for off she ran
With the same thought—and thus began.

"You, Doctor, as I understand,
Are fit to lead an opera band;

And, therefore, you may scarce incline
To add to such a crash as mine:
But if your powers will condescend
To treat me as a common friend,
You shall, Sir, in the evening try
My little school of harmony.
It is not oft 'mong ladies seen,
But I play on the violin.
To touch the harp and the piano
Is what each farmer's daughter can do;
And therefore 'tis I wish to move
With those who by their science prove
An honour to the art I love.
Hence my fond mind is solely bent
To chuse this arduous instrument.
I have a foreign person here,
Who at our dinner will appear,
A widow of the music tribe,
Whom I with handsome sal'ry bribe
To live with me in friendly guise,
As mistress of my harmonies:
She plays the bass, blows the bassoon,
And keeps the instruments in tune;
Teaches the parish boys to sing
Psalms, anthems, and God save the King."

Thus as she spoke a bugle's blast
Summon'd them to the hour's repast,
When she propos'd the famous glee
Of the Non Nobis Domine,
In which the ladies' parts were sung
Without or time, or tune, or tongue,
And Syntax felt, with all his care,
He should not pass his evening there;
That they would never keep in tune
Through the approaching afternoon;

For Music, with this mighty show,
Was the last thing they seem'd to know.
But still the good things he assail'd
Where Music's ev'ry form prevail'd,
That sing-song fancy could supply
To deck the skill of cookery,
Or the same whimsy could impart
To the confectionary art:
Thus songs in sav'ry wrappers shone
On cutlets *à la Maintenon*,
While *Blanc-mange* dotted o'er with notes,
Made Music slip adown their throats;
Then sweets in ev'ry form display
The instrumental orchestra:
Thus fiddles, flutes and harps unite
To harmonise the appetite.

   At length came the appointed hour
When, in the garden's gaudy bower,
Where flowers and climbing plants o'erlaid
Combin'd to form a scented shade,
These vot'ries of sweet sounds appear
To wake Apollo's list'ning ear.
—Miss C—— began with furious force,
The Doctor follow'd her of course,
While the old dame with slower pace,
Came rumbling after on the bass:
But ere they got to the conclusion,
Th' harmonious piece was all confusion.
If great Corelli from the dead
Could but have rais'd his list'ning head
And just then heard his mangled strain,
He would have wish'd to die again.
Miss was too fast by many a bar,
The old-one was behind as far,

THE GARDEN TRIO

While Syntax strove their faults to cover
By smoth'ring one and then the other.
"Oho," he whisper'd, "this same trio
Will shortly end in my *Addio*."
—He thought at least he would be civil
And try to check the coming evil;
For he saw in Miss Crotchet's face
That rage was working his disgrace.
"If Music be the food of love
Let us another trio prove,"
Syntax exclaim'd; when she replied,
"I tell you I am petrified;
To me, you humstrum, it appears,
That you have neither eyes nor ears;
You could as well bestride the moon,
As keep your time or stop in tune;
And 'twas, in an extreme degree,
Impertinence to play with me."
—Instead of *Time* he thought he'd beat,
With all good manners, a retreat;
But, in retiring from the threat,
With which he thought he was beset,
He overturn'd the o'ergrown fiddle,
And set his foot plump in the middle:
The crash produc'd a shriek of rage,
Which nought he utter'd could assuage,
When, to avoid the rout and roar,
He quickly pass'd the mansion door,
And, driven by *Discord*, sought to fly
From this strange scene of harmony,
While, with vociferating halloo,
He call'd on his man Pat to follow.
But Pat had half an hour's stay,
Before he told of his delay,
Which he let loose in his droll way.

—"The lady, Sir, 'tis very sad,
Is, I am sure, at times, half-mad!
She rush'd into the servants' hall
And utter'd, with an angry squall,
'Your master is a brute, I say,
And I have sent the fool away.'
'No *man*,' I said, 'would call him so,
But this arm's vengeance he should know,
Though as he's gone, why I must go!'
Orders she gave to lock the door,
And pointing wildly to the floor,
'Stand here,' she said, 'and sing a song,
Or you shall stop the whole night long.'
I bow'd and did at once let fly
A pretty piece of melody,
Such as did never yet miscarry
To please the lads of Tipperary:
The chamber madams whisper'd—Hush!
And knew not if to laugh or blush;
While the cook dame, call'd laughing Nan,
Beat time upon the dripping-pan.
The butler turn'd his head away,
So how he look'd I cannot say;
While stiff the little Negro stood,
Show'd his white teeth and grinn'd aloud.
—At the fourth verse off Madam flew,
And here, Sir, I'm return'd to you."

The Doctor now could not beguile
His feelings with his usual smile,
But lean'd his head against a tree,
And, spite of cleric dignity,
Let his gay muscles off at score,
As Pat ne'er saw him do before:
But when his spirits had regain'd
The gen'ral tenor they maintain'd,

He bade Pat ask how far from hence
Was Lady *Macnight's* residence;
"I know 'tis somewhere here about,
And we must try to find it out.
She's cousin to my friends the *Hearties*,
And sometimes join'd their pleasant parties.
Three years must now have flown away,
When, if I ever pass'd this way,
I promis'd I would show my face,
With her kind leave, at *Comet Place*."
A peasant said the road was strait,
And nine miles from the turnpike-gate;
But as the moon began to peep
Above the wood on yonder steep,
It would be soon as light as day,
And they could never lose their way.
"But as 'tis late," the Doctor said,
"Our journey must not be delay'd;
Though for this fair Astronomer,
Night is the time to visit her,
While she may chase through fields of air
The aberration of a star."
Punch felt the tickling of a spur,
And Pat's fat sides were in a stir:
Nor was it long ere, from the road,
They hail'd the lady's fair abode
That, plac'd upon a woody height,
Display'd full many a glimm'ring light,
Which from the various windows shone
And check'd the lustre of the moon.

The Doctor now made known his name,
When soon appear'd the smiling dame.
"I scarce, dear Sir, my joy can measure
At this so unexpected pleasure;

And 'tis with singular delight
I see my learned friend to-night."
Thus she exclaim'd, when Syntax fear'd
That some celestial sign appear'd,
And stead of supper and a bed
Whereon to lay his aching head,
He should be hurried to survey
The greater BEAR or MILKY WAY;
But thus she did his fears allay:
"Whene'er the moon shows all her power
And shines through each nocturnal hour,
My distant neighbours always come
As her clear beams will light them home,
And I have now a pleasant party
Which only wants my *Cousin Hearty*,
Though as you're come I'm quite content,
Without a word of compliment."

The Doctor soon in pleasant mood,
Amid the gay assembly stood:
Curtsies and bows and shaking hands
With all that etiquette demands
Pass'd on with due becoming grace,
Engaging words and smiling face.
The Doctor talk'd and sipp'd his tea
With pleasing, mild hilarity;
Nor did he fail a meal to make
On butter'd bread and sav'ry cake.
This done, the patronising dame
Propos'd some lively, gen'ral game;
And Syntax drew his ready chair
In the night's play to take a share.
Pope Joan was nam'd and soon prepar'd:
When each receiv'd the destin'd card.
The comely fair by whom he sat,
A lady cheerful in her chat,

DR SYNTAX AT A CARD PARTY.

Propos'd by way of social whim
To share the gain and loss with him.
Who could refuse a pleas'd assent?
And all around there beam'd content.
The game, in gen'ral way, went on,
And Syntax thought they rather won:
But still the lady often cried,
"Doctor, our wants must be supplied,
Fortune, at present, is unkind,
And we, dear Sir, must raise the wind."
He thought, indeed, he rais'd enough,
While she ne'er gave a single puff,
But of the cash maintain'd control
And in her lap conceal'd the whole.
At length when this gay game was o'er,
She said, "Alas, we're wond'rous poor,
And to propose to make division
Of what is here would be derision."
Then from her lap, which seem'd half full,
She almost fill'd her reticule,
And left the Sage, with silent lips,
To comment on copartnerships;—
While she stalk'd off with waving plume
To wander through some distant room.
—The supper came and pass'd away,
With many a song and frolic gay;
And when the household clock struck *one*,
The country neighbours all were gone.
—But ere the chamber lights were brought,
The scientific dame besought
The Doctor's patience to bestow
His ear for half an hour or so,
While she inform'd him by the way
Of the great object of the day.
"For you must know," she said, "at noon,
O'er the sun's disk the errant moon

Will pass, as that orb has not done
For many a year long fled and gone;
And, in this state of her career,
How I rejoice to see you here,
As you will aid my measuring eye
By your more learn'd Geometry.
That done, we then may pass the day
In tracing out some starry way;
And if it proves a radiant night
You'll set my computations right;
When, to conclude, I will make known
A system new and quite my own."
—The Doctor's chin now touch'd his breast:
She bow'd—and they both went to rest.

The morrow in due progress came,
When Syntax by th' impatient dame
Was led, not to the upper story
Which form'd her fix'd observatory,
Where many an instrument appears,
As quadrants, telescopes and spheres,
To aid the scrutinising eye
In its vast commerce with the sky:
But did in a balcony place
The glass, where she as well could trace
The lunar passage o'er the sun
As could from greater height be done.
—At length arriv'd the pregnant noon,
When o'er the sun the darken'd moon
Mov'd on the grand eclipse and show'd
What man to daring science ow'd.
But though the mind may strive to trace
The orbs that float in boundless space,
Though it may pass through realms of air,
Converse with planets rolling there
And, by its name call ev'ry star;

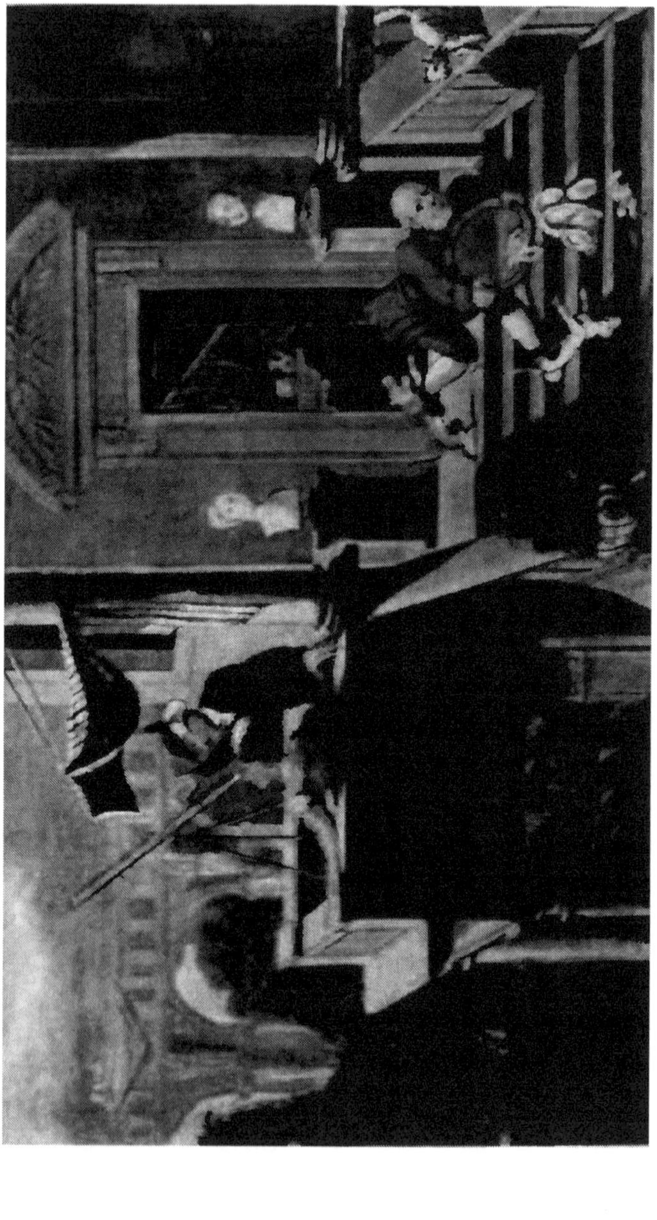

The body ne'er will be content
Without its native nourishment;
And hunger will suggest the sign
Of when to breakfast, sup or dine,
Or when the luncheon should reveal
Its interlocutory meal.
That meal, by frequent signals sought,
Pat now in eager hurry brought:
But whether 'twas the slipp'ry floor,
Or running dog, or banging door,
It may not be required to tell;
Certain it is the valet fell,
Swore a loud oath, when plate and platter
And spoons and sauce-boats made a clatter;
While yelping curs, or kick'd or wounded,
Were in the gen'ral din confounded;
A noise which both the gazers drew
From their celestial interview.
They saw, by Patrick's luckless trips,
The luncheon in complete eclipse,
As his huge form was rolling over
Each dainty dish and smoking cover,
While down his skirts there seem'd to stray
Fresh streamlets of the milky way.
"—The scene around, above, below,"
The Doctor said, "our problems show,
Whether it is attractive power,
Or the repellent rules the hour:
Patrick we see could not resist,
Or with his feet or with his fist:
His feet gave way, the balance lost,
His paunch to right and left is tost;
The fingers driven from the thumb
Make the tureen a *vacuum*:
And there we see the varlet lie,
A proof of *Central Gravity*."

Madam replied, "O never mind,
A fresh supply we soon shall find,
And, as when Falstaff cried peccavi,
We'll change the *gravity* for *gravy*.[1]
Nature hates *vacuums*, as you know,
We therefore will descend below,
And fill, with dainties nice and light
The *vacuum* in your appetite."
—All this was done, as it might be,
On axioms of Philosophy;
When the grave lady thus requested:—
"As other matters are digested,
And we have now an hour to spare,
Let us each take our reas'ning chair,
Then talk of what we've seen and know
Of things above and things below,
And do you first your system show;
When you have done, my learn'd divine,
Then I will venture upon mine."

Syntax.

"When from the earth we lift our eye
To the vast concave of the sky,
We view it like a curtain spread
That shows the welcome morning red;
The noon with golden splendor bright,
And the dark veil that clothes the night:
Thus both the light and shade are given,
With all the varying scenes of Heaven.
But when we lose the sun's bright ray,
The gloomy night succeeds to day:
Again his flaming lustre burns,
And then the cheerful day returns:

---

[1] Shakespeare, *Henry the Fourth*, Second Part, Act I.-

Still we behold, as they appear,
The varying pictures of the year.
The morn may yield its splendid reign
To cloudy mists and pouring rain:
And oft the noon is overcast,
'Mid the black storm and lightning's blast;
While pitchy clouds obscure the night,
And quench the bright stars' glimm'ring light.
Then, to our eyes, the giant sun
His annual circuit seems to run
In one grand course, and his career
Assigns the day and forms the year;
But when his setting orb retires,
Or earth no more perceives his fires,
The moon presents her silver ray,
And kindly sheds a fainter day:
Yet still she keeps her monthly race
With various beams and changeful face.
—Each planet in its proper sphere
Does round its distant orbit steer;
While, with peculiar lustre crown'd,
They course a fix'd eternal round,
And, in th' immeasurable space,
They know no change of time or place;
But in their rise and their decline,
All with a foreign radiance shine.
Their brilliant beams are not their own,
But borrow'd of the parent sun,
From whom all nature doth inherit
That active and creating spirit
Which gives to life each aim and end,
Where'er his genial rays extend.
—Again we see the thousand stars,
Not rang'd in circles or in squares,
But proving with their various light
The Hand that made them Infinite.—

If such the harmony that reigns,
If thus the Almighty power ordains,
May not these orbs, which your faint eye
Sees fix'd in one eternal sky,
To which, as it may seem, is given
To shine in a remoter heaven,
Each as a sun its splendor give,
And other worlds the rays receive?
Around the zones of other skies,
Their moons may shine, may set and rise
To other globes which raise their pole,
Whose lands spread wide, whose oceans roll,
Whose mountains lift their lofty head,
And shape the valley's deepen'd bed,
With climates that may smile or frown,
To changes subject like our own;
Nay, in the space of air and sky,
Suns, moons and stars and earths may lie
Invisible to human eye,
E'en with the powers which have been given
To penetrate the paths of Heaven.
—The comet, whose resistless force
Asks cent'ries to complete its course,
I shall not follow as it flies,
Nor trace its eccentricities;
Nor speak of sun-beams which are fraught
With swiftness that out-travels thought,
But lost in wonder close my view,
And listen silently to you."
—He ceas'd, and now with conscious pride,
The scientific dame replied:

"You have with truth your system told,
But may I, Doctor, be so bold

To say, that you have said no more
Than many a one has done before;
Though not with such perspicuous sense,
Or the same pleasing eloquence.
—Yes, on my loaded shelves you see
Each volume on astronomy,
That has encreas'd the author's fame
With added honour to his name:
I have all instruments at hand
That this vast science may demand,
Which do their wond'rous aid supply
To make acquaintance with the sky;
But I new systems shall explore;
I wish to know a little more.—
—Perhaps, you'll say, 'tis whim or fun,
And that a woman's tongue must run;
Or that conceit or silly pride
Do my weak, friv'lous fancies guide;
Or that by something like defiance
To the establish'd rules of science,
To be held forth I thus may strive,
As the most learned dame alive;
If such your thoughts, I hope you'll find
Some reason soon to change your mind,
Or that disdainful of the fame
Which those *Blue-stocking* fair-ones claim,
Who confine their pretty fancies,
To poems, novels and romances,
Who take no flight, but are content
To steep their minds in sentiment:
I wish to soar a little higher
Than their fine, fangled thoughts aspire:
If this be your sagacious guess,
You prophesy with some success.
I only ask you to attend
With the calm candour of a friend,

At least, if you an error see,
You will not pass a harsh decree,
But treat it with humanity."

    The Doctor, not by intuition,
But by a feeling call'd suspicion,
Was on her subject led to fear
That the new doctrine he should hear
Might require a cautious sense,
To give his thoughts without offence.
Oft with *Blue-stockings* upon earth
Reason he found a source of mirth;
And e'en when Fancy play'd her tricks
He could a pleas'd attention fix:
But when *Blue-stockings* please to soar,
Where none had ever been before,
He rather trembled at the height
Which mark'd this lady's promis'd flight.
When such a one her notions shrouds
In regions far above the clouds,
While she does her pure æther quaff,
He might not check a sudden laugh,
Which certainly would not agree
With the most calm philosophy;
And thus whate'er she might discover,
He wish'd the dang'rous trial over.
Hence did he frame each future thought
To be with proper answers fraught,
And thus he hop'd he was prepar'd,
When ask'd, to offer his award.
—Such was his aim, and then he heard
The wonders which she now preferr'd.

LADY MACNIGHT.

"You have explain'd in language clear
Each planet's course as they appear,

As they appointed are to run
In their own orbits round the sun;
You travell'd in your airy car
To visit ev'ry ruling star,
And did not, for a moment, err
In marking their true character,
Nor in assigning each its place
In the immensity of space:
But here you stop, and nothing know
Beyond the glasses' RAREE-SHOW.
Men, whose renown'd and learned name
Irradiates the fields of fame,
With all their genius to explore,
Have indeed told us something more.
When Nature's laws lay hid in night,
NEWTON unveil'd new rays of light,
And gave the wond'ring world to see,
By his sublime Geometry,
Those hidden powers which he has shown
To act in Nature's unison:
But of those orbs which deck the sky,
Tho' view'd by his pervading eye,
He gave no local history.
Nor did he e'er pretend to tell
What BEINGS might within them dwell,
Their forms, their natures and their speech,
To what perfection they might reach,
And how their systematic powers
Differ from this same world of ours:
What are their plants and flowers and trees,
If they have running streams and seas,
And whether fleeting time appears
Like ours divided into years,
And if their years by lunar powers
Are form'd of months and day and hours:

Whether their life concludes by death,
Or if men die for want of breath:
And if to their fond hope is given
Another world, a future Heaven.
What do I gain, when I but see
These planets' eccentricity,
Unless my reason could pervade
For what wise purpose they were made?
—You'll laugh no doubt, and say I dream,
If I should now unfold my scheme,
And think, perhaps, that I may vie
With Bedlam in its lunacy.
But I, dear Sir, am not so bent
Upon my mind's experiment,
As to look grave if my excursion
Should minister to your diversion;
Nor does the thought make me uneasy
That some have fancied I was crazy.
—While my poor dear Sir John was living,
Whose soul, I trust, is now in Heaven,
Some booby, in a long hiatus,
Urg'd him to burn my *Apparatus*:
When he said, 'No!—While she maintains
Each due decorum, while she gains
Their warm regard to whom she's known,
And who her smiling friendship own;
While I her fond affection share
And feel her faithful, tender care;
While she to household rule attends,
And makes home pleasant to my friends,
What care I, as at early morn,
I urge the chase, with hound and horn,
Or cheer at night each jovial soul
With the full glass and flowing bowl,
If she employs her eager eye
To trace the wonders of the sky!

Yes wives there are, and not a few,
Who a more idle course pursue,
Nor is there one of those who shine
The votaries of fashion's shrine
Whom I would e'er exchange for mine.'
—Thus did my dear lamented Knight
Set the intruding fellow right:
And much I hope, good Sir, that you
May think my husband's praises true;
And they, I trust, who know me well
Will the same friendly story tell."

SYNTAX.

"They who have gravely trod the round
Of gen'ral science must have found
That trifles, nay, that whims have led,
When floating in a thinking head,
To quicken genius as it tries
The course of new discoveries:
E'en accident has made a stir
In brains of the philosopher.
A codling falling from a tree
Might fix the point of gravity:
Or house-maid's twirling of a mop
Might into NEWTON's cranium pop
The principle, by which was found
Whether the poles are flat or round.
And why, my Lady, may not you
Strike from your study something new,
And, what's still better, useful too?"

LADY MACNIGHT.

"With that benignant lib'ral spirit,
Which I well know that you inherit,
I'm sure your justice will not swerve
From any praise I may deserve:

Nor will you with harsh rigour blame
If I attempt too high an aim,
And strive those regions to explore
As none have ever done before,
But call me back to reason's lore;
And, if strange wanderings appear,
Restore me to my proper sphere.

"Now, in due order, to proceed,
Philosophers have all agreed,
That to each planet, in its sphere,
Our earth rolls on in prospect clear,
And, in great Nature's solar scheme,
They're seen by us, as we by them.
Nay from analogy 'tis thought,
Though not by fix'd experience taught,
That these are worlds and though unknown
May bear a likeness to our own,
Peopled with beings who fulfil,
Like us, the Almighty Maker's will,
To answer, in their destin'd station,
The wise design of their creation.
And now you'll hear my cunning guess
At what these several orbs possess,
With every animated feature
Of what I call their reas'ning nature,
As the prime power that may controul
The active impulse of the whole.
—Whether I reason from its name,
Or angry redness of its frame,
It matters not how they refer
To stamp its native character;
I still shall dare suppose that MARS
Is the continual seat of wars;
Not of arm'd military bands,
Whom the fierce, bloody sword commands,

IN SEARCH OF A WIFE

But, from the beggar to the king,
Contest must be for ev'ry thing;
Nay for a fortune or a rattle
That there must be a constant battle;
That hourly, individual strife
Is the grand principle of life.
No helm or breast-plate do they wear,
Nor do they sword or jav'lin bear,
But all their policy consists
In a concomitance of fists;
In the sharp, nimble fingers' raps,
Or the broad palm's redundant slaps.
—They cannot get a steak to eat
Unless they battle for the meat;
Nor can their statesmen get a place
'Till they have fought it face to face.
But then I'd have it understood
They never cause discharge of blood:
Whatever blows the parties give
Whatever bruises they receive,
A lasting pain they cannot feel,
And all without a plaister heal.
As bound by nature to oppose,
Friendship's an interchange of blows.
Fond lovers in their am'rous greeting
Know not of kissing or entreating,
'Tis done by scratching and by beating;
And love cannot be better shown
Than by a rude squeeze and a frown.
—Children and youth I shall suppose
Have not the privilege of blows,
Nor gain permission to engage
'Till they can prove they are of age.
—Of virtue contest is the source,
And moral rectitude is force;

While he who does the most contest
Is of the sons of MARS the best.
—Thus he, I'm ready to suppose,
Who ne'er receives nor offers blows,
Is an offender 'gainst the laws,
And subject to the hangman's paws,
Or sentenc'd to some dismal place
'Mong criminals who keep the peace;
And as we do our convicts see
Depriv'd of cheerful liberty,
They're chain'd in some dark cell below,
'Reft of the joy to strike a blow.—
—So far, so good—their power of speech
At present is beyond my reach :
Morals and manners form the whole
That's subject to my mind's controul,
And farther, Doctor, I confess,
It is not in my power to guess :
What my search may hereafter do,
As I my vent'rous course pursue,
I cannot say ;—but what say you ?"

SYNTAX.

"Nay Madam, you have gone as far,
Riding a cock-horse on a star,
Nay farther than has yet been known
By any Genius but your own :
—Indeed, I must admire your fancy,
In this star-gazing necromancy ;
For you have nat'ralis'd your sphere,
As I could ne'er expect to hear.—
Though with the plan I can't agree,
I thank you for its drollery ;
And though I cannot well allow
The principle which you avow,

Your story, Shakespeare gives the hint,
Though strange, has much of matter in't."

LADY MACNIGHT.

"A few words more and I have done
With these attendants on the sun.
—In the bright orb that's known to claim
VENUS as its establish'd name,
I shall pursue my arduous way
In the conjectures of the day,
That BEAUTY is the height sublime
Of *Virtue* in that genial clime,
Whose light and heat, within its zone,
Bears no resemblance to our own;
And the grand crime they there confess,
Is what we here term *Ugliness*.
The good and ill which there prevail
Is measur'd by a settled scale
Among its people, as each feature
Is favour'd or deform'd by nature;
And all the value of their duty
Is form'd by more or less of beauty;
And thus it is that I pervade
Its moral light, its moral shade.
—The flowing hair, the well-turn'd brow,
The fine form'd arches just below,
A skin that vies with driven snow:
The bright, the soft and sleepy eye,
The two-fold rows of ivory;
The pouting, ruby-colour'd lips,
Where sweetness its own nectar sips;
The checks with rosy blush o'erspread,
And dimples sinking in the red;
The neck that doth the bosom join
By a scarce seen but graceful line,

While the firm semi-orbs below
Heave with a gentle to and fro;
And arms whose less'ning round extends
To the fine, taper fingers' ends:—
—Such is the form, and such the grace,
That's virtue in the female race;
While man's proportions are the same,
But suited to a stronger frame.
Each virtue is, and more or less
They virtuous are, who most possess;
While the vicious nature lies
Proportion'd by its contraries.
Therefore it is that I suppose
The squinting eye, the wide-spread nose,
The yawning mouth, that may appear
Stretching athwart from ear to ear;
The rising back, a sad mischance,
And stomach's rude protuberance,
Are crimes which, by their law's intent,
Receive proportion'd punishment;
While ugliness in ev'ry sense,
Must be a capital offence;
And they will be comdemn'd to die,
Whose crime's complete deformity.
So much, dear Doctor, for my Venus,
And what as yet has pass'd between us."
—She paus'd—but when she 'gan to tell
Of Mercury, the dinner-bell
Brought her fine fancies to a close;
And as the Rev'rend Doctor rose
He said, " I here beg leave to mention
How much I'm pleas'd with your invention,
But still I think it might be right
To calm its course and check its flight,
Nor let it wander out of season,
But yield it to the rule of reason;

And instead of its commanding,
Let it obey, your understanding:
Consult your own superior sense,
And gratify your pride from thence:
For all is known we ought to know
Of things above, or things below,
'Till other Boyles and Newtons rise
T' unveil dark Nature's mysteries.
I do not strictly mean to say
You throw your studious hours away,
Or that your star-work is misspent,
For still the pastime's innocent;
But yet I think that *à la lettre*,
You might employ those hours better:
Nor do I wish to read a lecture
Upon the errors of conjecture,
Which may refinement's thoughts expose
To smiling friends and scoffing foes;
I only ask you to receive
The friendly counsel that I give:
If to the Planets you must soar,
Be silent, wonder and adore.
Though they're in diff'rent stations plac'd
In the immeasurable waste,
Though their ends may not be the same,
Each is to answer one great aim,
And with some local means endued,
To aid the universal good,
Will'd by the Power whose plastic hand
Doth all immensity command,
And whose vast, universal sway
Creation's countless worlds obey."

He spoke, and in due order pass'd,
To things more suited to his taste.

Indeed, he was well pleas'd to see
A change in the philosophy;
And with his knife and fork to reason
On ev'ry dainty dish in season,
And make his choice 'tween wrong and right,
As guided by his appetite.
At length the plenteous dinner o'er,
As he did in his goblet pour
The sparkling wine, he begg'd to give
A toast she surely would receive.
"Here's to the health of friends above,
I care not in what star they move,
Or whatso'er their modes may be;—
May they have din'd as well as we!"—
—The afternoon they stroll'd away,
In various chit-chat, grave and gay,
And time brought on the close of day;
When Syntax begg'd she would make known
"Any commands she had in town,
As early on the following day,
Thither he must direct his way."
"O," she replied, "I will commend
Your Rev'rence to my charming friend
Dear Mrs. BRISKIT, whom I've known
Since I was taught to walk alone.
In her I know that you will find
Good manners and a fashion'd mind:
But if she has a fault, Heav'n bless her,
'Tis the high spirits which possess her:
She'll laugh with you in endless glee
At my high flown Astronomy!
Though, as her husband's lately sent
On business to the Continent,
She sees 'till his return but few:
Yet this I know, with honour due,
Her door will open be to you.

IN SEARCH OF A WIFE

—And now I think on't there's another
To whom without or form or pother
I must, dear Doctor, introduce you:
O how that dear girl will amuse you!
My sweet Miss PALLET, she is one,
To whom, my friend, you must be known,
A female Artist, whose fair name
Is rising rapidly to fame,
And all the paintings round the room
Did from her earliest pencil come:
Her works you will with pleasure view,
Nay, you can give instruction too.
My fond hopes wait on her success,
As I was her first patroness;
And she my friendship will commend,
When I present her such a friend."

While she these kindly passports wrote,
He did the passing time devote
To a small volume, whose rich page
Would his delighted mind engage,
And when her scribbling work was done,
He thus his farewell thoughts made known:
"—As your pen mov'd, by chance I took
From off your shelves a fav'rite book,
Of solemn bards the boasted pride,
You know him well, 'tis AKENSIDE—
And in his high-wrought work you'll see }
Fancy rob'd in Philosophy,
What that pow'r is and ought to be; }
And in its page the Muses show
What Fancy does to Reason owe:
Nay, there a lesson may be known
How you, fair dame, may guide your own.
—And as my grateful thanks I tell,
And while I humbly say, farewell,

Your gracious kindness may receive
The faithful counsel which I give.—
Like poor Sir John's advising friend,
I would not dare to recommend
That you should venture to destroy
The apparatus you employ,
But lock the door of that high story,
Which forms your learn'd Observatory;
Against the stars at once rebel,
And throw the KEY into a WELL."

CANTO XXXVII

SYNTAX, in deep, and pensive mood,
  Tow'rds London now his way pursued:
The eastern sky involv'd in cloud
Did from his eye the sun-beams shroud,
And not one active darting ray
Gave spirit to the early day:
While the mist, hanging o'er the brow
Of woody upland, sunk below
Amid the smoke, rais'd on the gale,
From hamlet cottage in the vale.—
No lark was heard, ascending high,
To give his carol to the sky;
Nor did the blackbird or the thrush
Make vocal the green, dewy bush:
The rooks, departing from the wood,
On the high branches cawing stood,
Whose noisy notes alone were heard,
With raven's croak, ill-omen'd bird,
And gloomy nature's self gave warning
Of a dull, uninspiring morning,
At least, of thoughts alive and gay,
Which sometimes flow from radiant day.
What was the cause doth not appear;
Whether oppressive atmosphere,
Or that the pillow had not blest
The Doctor with his usual rest;

Or whether it was fancy's whim,
(Which seldom rul'd or troubled him,)
He was not in his usual trim;
So that he, as he ponder'd o'er
The dark side of his nuptial Tour,
Had half a mind to turn again
To the green shades of Sommerden,
And be contented with the good
Which he might find in widowhood.
"Since I left home," he mutt'ring said,
"What to my wish has been display'd?
The high-flown fair whom I have sought
Did not awake one tender thought:
Such sense mix'd up with so much folly
At times would make me melancholy:—
They might, perchance, an hour, a day,
Contrive to pass in smiles away,
But Fortune I should ne'er forgive,
If I with such were doom'd to live.
—It is not that a woman's mind
May not be of superior kind,
Or that its powers may not be fraught
With views enlarg'd and depth of thought,
Or that a lady's studious hours
May not have treasur'd learning's stores:
I know that many have been known,
Who in the realms of science shone,
Whose learning, judgment, critic taste,
Have seldom been by men surpass'd,
And yet who never soar'd above
The line where duty bade them move,
And were not seen to give offence
To that prime virtue, COMMON-SENSE.
But these are form'd for higher life
And not to be a parson's wife,

Unless by fortune he had been
A bishop, or at least a dean,
Whose dames, thus living at their ease,
May chuse what pastime they shall please."

The clouds now broke and many a ray
Of sunshine darted on the day;
When, as inspiring Phœbus shone,
The Doctor chang'd his grumbling tone,
While a good breakfast had the merit
To quicken his dejected spirit;
And now his homeward way to trace
He thought would be downright disgrace;
That perseverance was a feature
Which aggrandis'd our common nature:
And no great act he could relate,
Of ancient or of modern date,
But to that virtue did refer
Its energetic character.
Thus, without further doubt or fear,
He was resolv'd to persevere.—
Nay, as his spirits 'gan to rise,
He ventur'd to soliloquise,
And did his waken'd hopes express,
Of what he thought he might possess.

"LONDON is the general mart,
The warehouse vast that does impart
Whate'er the life of man requires,
To minister to its desires:
But mine's a search of tender feeling;—
Those articles I cannot deal in
Which demand a golden treasure
To furnish out luxurious pleasure,
To gratify each active sense,
Or love of proud magnificence;

These come not in my humble view,
They are not what my thoughts pursue:
I've but a faithful heart to offer,
And a warm parson's home to proffer,
Where a fond pair may love and live,
Though this is all I have to give,
Yet I shall think it rather hard
If, as my errant toil's reward,
I cannot find a Ma'am or Miss
Somewhere in this metropolis,
Who may indulge a secret wish
To dip her sop in Hymen's dish;
Who'd like to leave its noisy riot,
To live with me in rural quiet.
But after all if I should fail,
And all my hostile stars prevail,
I will not my false hopes lament,
But teach my mind to be content,
Contrive to cheer my widow'd life
Without the blessing of a wife,
And while I live, I ne'er again
Will leave the woods of Sommerden."
—Such were the thoughts, from day to day,
Which beguil'd his untroubled way,
'Till rising 'bove the cloud of smoke
St. Paul's Dome on the prospect broke;
And, pacing on, he enter'd town
By the north side of Mary-bonne.
A proper inn he sought of course,
Where there was food for man and horse,
'Till he could find a decent station
In point of air and situation,
As it might most convenient seem,
And fitted to his leading scheme.
Thus as he trotted through a street,
Whose houses seem'd compact and neat,

Apartments to be let was seen
Upon a door of brightest green,
And underneath a name had place,
As dealer in fine foreign lace:
The curtain'd windows caught the eye,
With their gay, festoon'd drapery,
And in balconies there were seen
Flowers and plants of ever-green,
Where the geraniums blossom'd red,
And myrtles rose from mossy bed,
While all, as far as he could see,
Appear'd to suit him to a T.
—He thought what trouble it would save,
If here he could a lodging have;
So he knock'd smartly at the door
And was admitted to explore
The diff'rent rooms by a fat lady,
Who certainly was pass'd her heigh-day,
But if time had destroy'd her figure,
Her tongue retain'd its pristine vigour;
Thus she so manag'd to succeed
By flatt'ring chat, that he agreed
No other residence to seek,
And took th' apartments for a week.
He answer'd to the usual claim,
And paid a pound note to the dame;
Deliver'd his portmanteau there,
To the old lady's promis'd care,
Then took his leave with spirits light
And promis'd to be there at night.
PAT too receiv'd commands to find
A liv'ry stable to his mind,
Where both the travell'd nags and he
Might find due hospitality;
And bade him keep it in his pate
To be with him next morn at eight.

"Well, now," said Syntax, "I'll e'en go
And visit *Pater-noster-Row*,
VELLUM I trust will much rejoice
To hear once more my well-known voice."
He went, and as St. Paul's struck three,
His appetite rejoic'd to see
The print and paper-selling sinner
Preparing for a plenteous dinner.
—After much warm and friendly greeting
At this so unexpected meeting,
When the good Doctor's hungry zeal
Was settled by a hearty meal,
While a full pint of wine at least,
Had given spirits to the feast,
Vellum his curious talk began,
To dip into the Doctor's plan,
And by his shrewd discourse discover
What just now made him such a rover.
"—You cannot have been long in town,
Or some Muse with the news had flown
And have contriv'd to let us know
The pleasing tidings in the *Row*:
For you, no doubt Sir, must have brought
Some work with taste and learning fraught,
Something of bold and new design,
Dug from the never-failing mine
That's work'd within your fertile brain,
Where all is cut and come again;
And much I hope you will command
My practis'd and obstetric hand,
And chuse me, as my skill you know,
Among the midwives of the *Row*,
To bring it forth, with your fair name,
To a long, future life of fame."
A smile now seem'd to give assent,
And Vellum's visage beam'd content:

But when he from the Doctor heard,
What street and place he had preferr'd,
And that he was thus lodg'd alone
In a snug house in Mary-bonne,
He thought without a smile or joke
He should speak out—and thus he spoke.
"—Where'er you are there must be good,
Whate'er may be the neighbourhood;
But, 'tis a region, let me say,
Where you, Sir, will not wish to stay,
Though I do not presume to measure
Either your fancy or your pleasure:
But should you wish to quit the place,
Which possibly may be the case,
I have a friend who has left town
For sev'ral months, and who does own
Nice chambers in an Inn of Court,
Where Sages of the Law resort;
And he has left, as you may see,
The entire care of them to me,
Furnish'd with all accommodation
That well may suit your rev'rend station;
And where you may employ your pen,
As quiet as at *Sommerden*,
With a neat laundress to attend you,
To whose good care I should commend you."
Said Syntax, "In a day or two,
I'll ask another interview,
And then the subject we'll renew."
—The hasty evening pass'd away
On gen'ral topics of the day;
How learning sped was not neglected,
And authors of all kinds dissected;
'Till the departing hour was come,
And Syntax sought his novel home

To the opening door there came
The old, fat, grinning, prating dame,
Who begg'd that he would take a chair
In her boudoir, and seat him there:
Smart, well dress'd, giggling Misses three,
Compos'd the old lady's company.
"These, I presume, these charming fair,"
He said, "are your maternal care?"
"These are my chicks," the dame replied,
"At once my profit and my pride,
Some folks have talk'd about their beauty,
But this I know, they do their duty,
And e'en if scandal dare to flout 'em,
I'm sure I could not do without 'em."
But with his day's fatigue oppress'd,
Syntax begg'd leave to go to rest.
"Laura," she said, " I prithee come,
And light the Doctor to his room."
She rose and as she squeez'd his arm
He calmly smil'd, but thought no harm ;
He took it in the kindest sense,
And thought it frolic innocence;
Bore, from her hand the blazing light,
Then bade God bless her and good night.

He was next morn in full array
And planning out the future day,
When Pat appear'd quite pale and wan,
And thus in ruffled tones began:
"I hope you will not take offence
If I just tell your Reverence,
This is a house of evil fame,
I know its character and name:
A coach is here—Be off, I pray,
Nor here another minute stay;

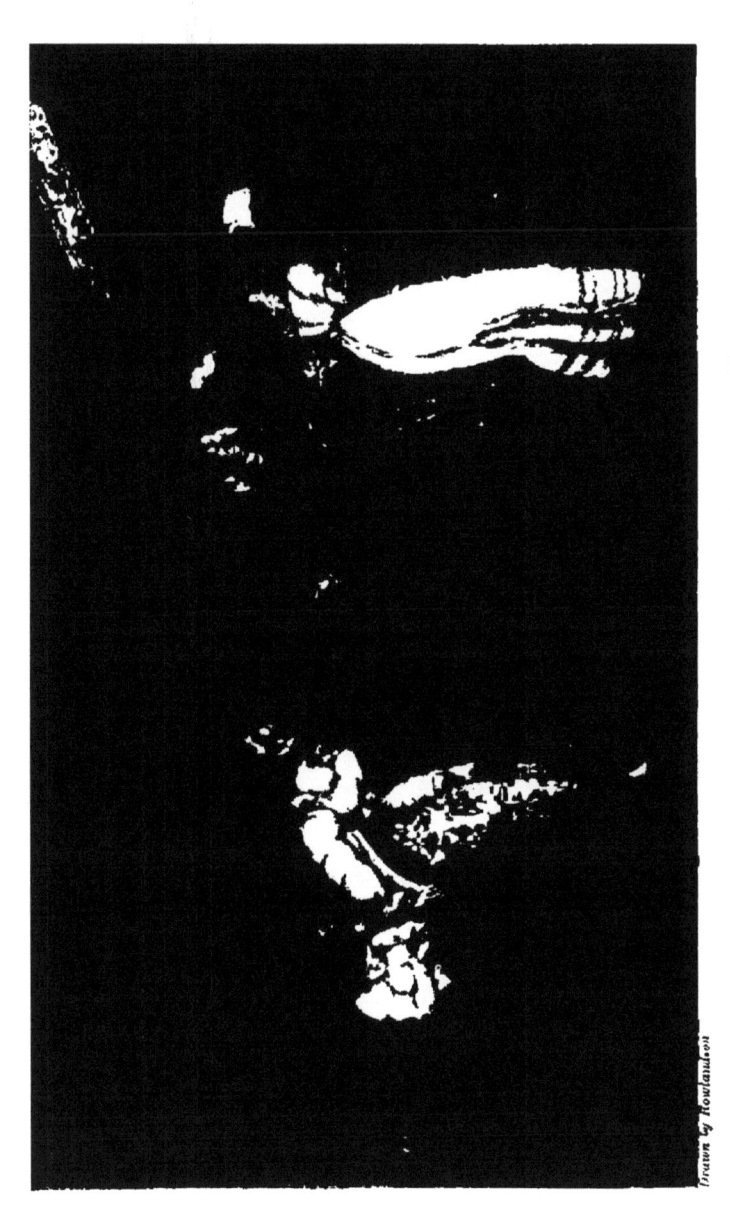

Dr SYNTAX IN THE WRONG LODGING HOUSE.

Drawn by Rowlandson

You now, Sir, may remove in quiet,
Or the old hag will breed a riot."
Nay, now, from what we saw last night,
The Doctor thought that Pat was right,
Who soon the trav'lling baggage bore
Strait to the hackney at the door;
And then flew back to save his master
From any insolent disaster:
But, as the staircase he descended,
He found the passage well defended.
There the hag stood, all hubber-bubber,
A half-dress'd form of living blubber.
"What going, Sir, without a warning?"
"Yes," Syntax said, "and so good-morning."
"But stop, Sir, pray, and hear me speak;—
You still must pay me for a week."
"One pound," says Pat, "for one night's rent,
Is pay enough, so be content."
But she by some outlandish name
Bawl'd, "Captain come!"—The Captain came,
When he display'd a horrid grin,
More frightful from his hairy chin,
And threaten'd loud; but Patrick stood,
In a stout, sturdy attitude.
"Ah, move," he said, "and you shall feel
That Paddy has a heart of steel;
Nay, Captain, he may prove to you,
That he has hands of iron too."
Whether the Captain did not like
The kind of blows that Pat might strike,
With mumbling oaths and ghastly frown,
He went up-stairs as he came down.
Thus neither light nor heavy-hearted,
But between both the Sage departed;
Though not o'erburden'd with content,
To Vellum now again he went.

There are, and many I have known,
Though not to naughty habits prone,
Who are scarce ever heard to swear,
And seldom miss their Sunday prayer,
Yet of their lively rovings boast,
When youthful fancies rul'd the roast;
And while their latter days prevail,
Or o'er their wine, or punch, or ale,
And while the smoking fume ascends
Among familiar, social friends,
Will chuckle at an idle thought,
Which Scandal's gossip tongue has brought,
And cautious looking round the while,
Will give the half corrected smile.
Such solemn Vellum was, and when
Syntax he saw so soon again,
That Mary-bonne, a shrewd guess told him,
The Doctor found too hot to hold him.
—But though our fanciful Divine
Ne'er thought to play the libertine,
He could not, as he sipp'd his tea,
Refrain from mystic drollery,
And by that drollery did provoke
The Bookseller to cut a joke,
And, with a blinking eye, let fall
Quaint words in sense equivocal.
—But now, to cut the matter short,
Nice Chambers in an Inn of Court
Receiv'd the Sage that very night,
And there he found that all was right;
With Laundress ready to attend
His service as an humble friend.
The travelling steeds at liv'ry stood
Somewhere in the near neighbourhood,
So that Pat ever was at hand,
For any duty at command.

IN SEARCH OF A WIFE

—In thought the morrow was employ'd,
Which, as it pass'd, was not enjoy'd;
For he began to think his scheme
Was but an idle, fruitless dream,
While reason, in this state of doubt,
Seem'd not dispos'd to help him out.
In ev'ry shape the cause he tried,
But still he was not satisfied.
Thus as he pac'd from room to room,
Contemplating his future doom,
With scarce a hope his mind to cheer,
And yielding to a coward fear;
"Is it that I a place have chose,"
He gravely said, "where life's worst foes
Their unpropitious gains receive,
From eyes that weep and hearts that grieve?
Is it that I with Lawyers share
This dismal roof, this tainted air,
That I an humble spirit bear,
And seem no longer to preserve
The active mind, the daring nerve;
Nay, am at once dispos'd to yield
The conquests of the promis'd field?"
Thus as he spoke, good Mrs. Broom,
The Laundress, came into the room,
And hearing how he talk'd and sigh'd,
Thus in respectful tone replied.
"Believe me in this staircase here,
I've pass'd, good Sir, full many a year;
And I have many a Lawyer serv'd
Who ne'er from truth or justice swerv'd;
Though, Sir, perhaps, within this court
There may be some of ev'ry sort:
But if you chose to change the air,
For Portland-place or Portland-square,
Of those who live in splendour there

I fear that you might say the same
Nor do injustice to their name.
Some vile professor of the Laws
Has grip'd you hard within his paws,
I must suppose, and given you cause
The common anger to sustain
Against the Laws and Lawyers' train.
Excuse me, Sir, but I must smile
At whims that do our minds beguile.
I met just now, upon the stairs,
A Dandy in his highest airs,
Who calls the Lawyer that's above
The faithful clerk of doating love;
And swears that by his powerful pen
He proves himself the best of men.
Though, Sir, if I must speak the truth,
This gallant and delighted youth
Is on the lawyer's toil intent,
Whose skill draws up an instrument,
Which, when in all due form prepar'd,
Will give him his vast love's reward:
O 'tis a most delicious sound
Beauty, and forty thousand pound!"
The Doctor smil'd nor check'd the dame,
Who thus continued to exclaim;
"Marriage I think, as well I know,
Is the far happiest state below;
I twice have prov'd that happy state;
Twice I have lost a faithful mate,
Nor do I think it yet too late,
To seek again love's soft dominion,
Were John Quill-drive of my opinion."

This chatter, and of marriage too,
Brought the same subject to the view

Of Syntax in a better state
Than he had given it thought of late:
Besides, good wine and dainty fare
Are sometimes known to lighten care:
Nay, man is often brisk or dull
As the keen stomach's void or full.
The Doctor, to all meals inclin'd,
Had on a well-dress'd sweet-bread din'd,
While a nice pie of sav'ry meat
Gave added poignance to the treat;
As the good Laundress wish'd to show,
That she did kitchen cunning know,
And, therefore, had contriv'd the best
To furnish out a tempting feast:
While Vellum had Madeira sent
Which might a Bacchanal content.
He ate, he drank, his spirits rose,
And cheerful thoughts succeed to those
Which through the hopeless morning past,
Had his shrunk mind with doubts o'ercast.
—Again he pac'd the chamber floor,
And talk'd his various projects o'er.—
" E'en should they fail he knew no harm,
That ought to give his mind alarm:
The smiles of Fortune, if attain'd,
Must be by perseverance gain'd;
Therefore, be gone, thou Coward, Fear,
For Syntax still shall persevere."

Thus as these thoughts his spirits cheer'd
Vellum with smile and bow appear'd;
" I come to know, Sir, if you find
The situation to your mind;
And if ought can be added to it
I trust that you will let me know it;

For you shall see it is my pride
To have it instantly supplied."
The Doctor fail'd not in expressing
His thanks for all he was possessing.
—Now Vellum had a ready nose
For scenting works, in verse or prose,
Which Authors, for some special reason,
Might keep a secret for a season:
Authors, we mean, whose favour'd name,
Is trumpeted by Madam Fame.
A dinner he was us'd to try,
With a few scraps of flattery:
Of wealth and gen'rous deeds would boast,
A theme on Authors seldom lost;
And these, kept up with prudent skill,
Might bring the Author to his will.
Hence may be trac'd the worldly feeling
That brought on all this friendly dealing;
For surely Vellum could not dream
But that it was some learned scheme
Which brought the Doctor up to town,
When all the show of life was flown.
Syntax, with native keenness felt
At what the cunning tradesman spelt;
At the same time he did not feel
It would be prudent to reveal
The curious wish that bade him roam
So far in summer months from home;
But to avert his prying eye
The Sage began this colloquy:—
"You have already had a ken
Of what I call a specimen,
When piety inspir'd my pen,
And much, my friend, I wish to know,
Could I a pious volume show,

All fair and ready for the press,
What you may think of its success,
And as we both may be concern'd,
If fame and money may be earn'd?"
 V. "What mean you?—Sermons?"—S. "Yes,
  the same."
 V. "Sermons by you, and with your name:—
Upon a first and gen'ral view,
I rather think that they will do:
At all events, Sir, as a friend,
I to your int'rests will attend."

 Thus with solemn face he spoke,
And we will guess, by way of joke
What to himself Old Vellum said,
As the sly, secret hints of trade.
Deep thought two forehead wrinkles prov'd,
But neither tongue nor lips were mov'd,
While to his interests never blind,
These hints were whisper'd to his mind:

 "Sermons by him!—O quite the thing,
To publish in the ensuing spring!
They will I'm sure be all the fashion,
And read, perhaps, by half the nation.
For Sermons, as the taste prevails,
Are read as eagerly as tales,
And if the preacher has renown
No works more popular are known.
I'll try to-morrow ere we dine
To fix the copy-right as mine."
But still he thought: "Why need I stay,
To strike this stroke, another day!
Another day? No, No—I vow
I'll strive to make the bargain now."

Thus these dumb hopes acquired strength,
So that he let them speak at length,
But in a calm and measur'd tone :—
"—These Sermons, Doctor, I must own
I rather wish "——" My honest friend,"
Syntax exclaim'd, " I must attend
To other matters which, 'tis known,
Have caus'd my pilgrimage to town;
And it will be a week or two
Before I can attend to you:
But, sure I am—it cannot be
That we should ever disagree."

Vellum, well pleas'd that he had made
Some progress in the way of trade,
Which, as he plann'd it, would repay
All his shrewd sense could do or say,
His sly enquiries now repress'd,
And hush'd his wary zeal to rest:
Thus, having smok'd a pipe or two
In social mood, he bade adieu.

Syntax, who had not liv'd so long
Without that sense of right and wrong,
Which Observation's known to give
To those who think as well as live,
Felt Vellum's use—but then he knew
That int'rest must be kept in view;
That this same money-scraping sinner
Would ne'er be lur'd to give a dinner,
Nor would his spirit e'er incline
To ask a *Letter'd Man* to dine,
Or bow, or smile, or send his wine,
Unless he thought by way of trade,
His kindness would be well repaid.
He therefore kept 'neath lock and key
These Volumes of Divinity;

And did his distant promise make,
To keep curmudgeon zeal awake.
—Thus it appears the day was pass'd,
And night's calm hour arriv'd at last;
For, Vellum and the Laundress gone,
The Doctor now was left alone;
As Pat took up his night's abode
Where Punch with her companions stood,
And moisten'd many a Dublin tale
With the rich draughts of London ale.
But Syntax, ere he went to rest,
Ponder'd on what might be the best,
What it became him now to do,
And which the way he should pursue.
"Can I," he calmly said, "do better,
Than send my Lady *Macknight's* letter?
And thus fair Mrs. BRISKIT see
With all her wild vivacity,
Nor fear the risk what she may do
With all her fun and frolic too."
Thus, the next morn, a formal note
He with all due politeness wrote,
To let her know what joy 'twould give him,
Did she but say she would receive him."
"—This evening *Madcap* is at home,"
The answer said, "so prithee come."—
"How," she exclaim'd, "shall I enjoy,
The visit of this Rev'rend Boy!
I shall be in my highest sphere,
When the Quixotic Parson's here!"
No sooner was it said than done,
And thus commenc'd the scheme of fun.
All in due time a stout house-maid
Was like the lady's self array'd;
The pendants dangle from her ears,
The plumage o'er her brow appears;

The ostrich spoils, so green, so red,
Bent graceful from her auburn head,
While all that pucker'd silk could show
Appear'd in flounce and furbelow,
And muslin's border'd folds display'd
The pow'rs of millinery aid.
The *Reticule* grac'd one rude hand,
The other did a fan command;
But Molly, in this tonish dress,
Was the sublime of awkwardness.
While she, indeed, or sat or stood,
All motionless as log of wood,
She look'd like wholesome flesh and blood;
But when she mov'd and when she spoke,
Then was to come the promis'd joke,
As Syntax, by the trick betray'd,
Would for the mistress take the maid,
And let forth many a classic speech,
Which pedant gallantry might teach;
While Madam, from some cushion'd height,
Not seen, nor yet quite out of sight,
Could from behind a curtain's sweep
With silent caution take a peep,
At the cross-purposes display'd
'Tween Syntax and the lady-maid:
But when the parley awkward grew
She might at once appear to view,
And in brisk measure rush between
To give new spirit to the scene.
Such was the plan this lively dame
Had laid to form the evening's game,
And in due course the evening came.

   Pat now applied his utmost art
To make his Rev'rend Master smart,

Who when he cast a partial eye,
The smooth-fac'd mirror passing by,
Just whisper'd, on the glancing view,
"'Tis not amiss—I think 'twill do.
And now," he said, "'twere well to try
A taste of that electuary,
Which, as I've known, so often serves
To give fresh vigour to the nerves."
He with the dose was well content,
For 'twas of that which Vellum sent.

Now in a hack was Syntax shook,
And Pat behind his station took,
When thus, in all becoming state,
They pass'd along through Gray's Inn Gate.
—The Doctor let his fancy bend,
As to the evening he should spend;
And how he might be best prepar'd
To play a safe and cautious card;
For sure he was from all he knew,
There would be fun and frolic too;
But what this gamesome Ma'am would do
His mental eye could not foresee,
Though in such near futurity.—
Thus as he conn'd his lesson o'er,
The carriage reach'd the promis'd door.
—In the mean time the bouncing maid
Was taught the part that should be play'd;
And thus the artful Mistress gave
Th' instruction how she should behave.
"When he shall ask you how you do,
You'll say, I'm well and thank you too.
But beyond this you must not go,
Nor e'er reply but YES or NO."
What other fancies she was told
A few lines onward will unfold.

He enter'd, when with awkward air
She motion'd him to take a chair,
And, having plac'd it by her side,
He thus began—She thus replied:—
"Ma'am, 'tis an honour you confer"—
She said—"*I'm well and thank you Sir.*"
"—I have a letter here to show
From Lady Macnight"—She said, "*No.*"
"—I hope you'll take it not amiss,
If I present it!"—She said, "*Yes.*"
"I'm Doctor Syntax as I live."
She answer'd with a *Negative.*
O ho! he thought, but I'll go on,
For Madam I suppose for fun
Is playing an Automaton;
And if that is the Lady's cue,
I will be somewhat funny too.
"Madam," he said, "that lovely face
Seems to invite a soft embrace,
And if you please"—She answer'd, "*Yes.*"
The Doctor therefore took a kiss,
Which she return'd with such a blow
As her rude hands could well bestow:
But while, astonish'd and amaz'd,
He on the angry figure gaz'd,
The Lady thought it time to move
From her snug hiding-place above:
Into the room at once she darted;
The Doctor turn'd around and started,
And, scarce recov'ring from the slap,
Sunk unawares in Molly's lap.
She shov'd him briskly tow'rds the dame,
Who push'd him back from whence he came,
And thus, by force of arms uncouth,
He play'd at to and fro with both;

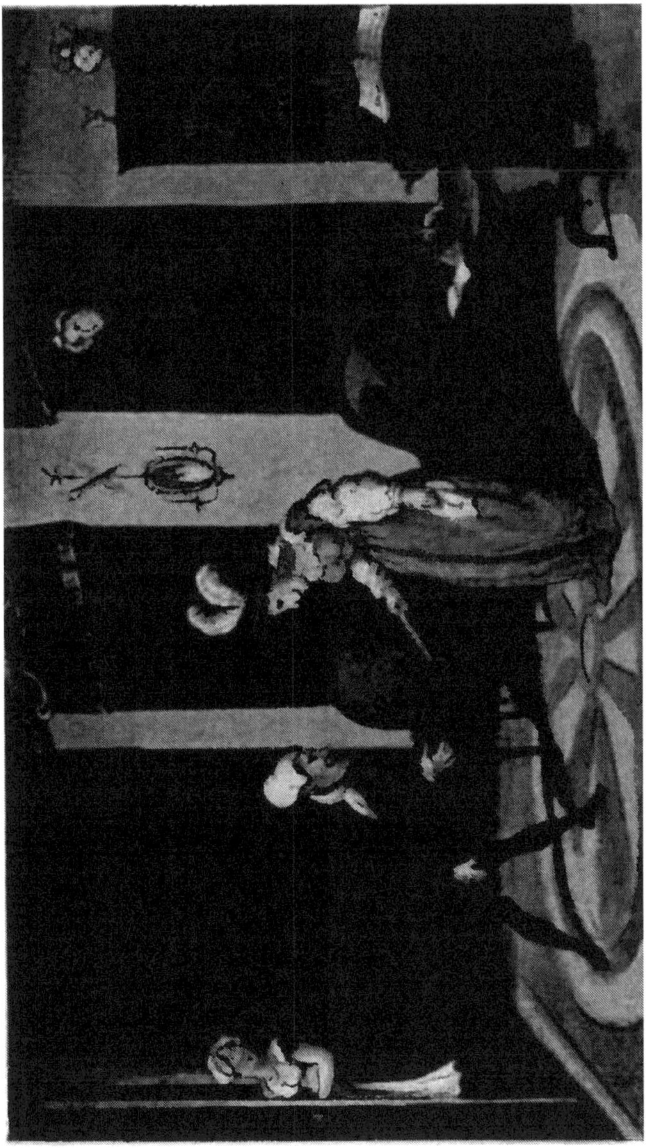

Such as a shuttlecock explores,
Between two active battledores.
—Molly, who thought her bus'ness o'er,
Made hasty passage through the door,
And left the Madcap Madam Briskit
With her sage, rev'rend beau to frisk it.
—But now another air prevail'd,
When she her visitor assail'd
With humble grace and winning smile,
So form'd displeasure to beguile;
And, having kindly grasp'd his hand,
With looks not easy to withstand:
"I am," she said, "a silly creature,
And you, I know, are all good nature,
Which will without offence receive
The droll reception that I give.
'Tis thus I ever treat my friends,
But I will make you full amends:
For though the evening has begun
In gamesome play and active fun,
Reason shall better things supply,
And all shall end in harmony."
—The Lady did her promise keep,
Her gambol spirits went to sleep:
And in whate'er she did or said
Such serious goodness was display'd,
So pleasing to his ear and eye,
As well as reverend dignity,
So subject to sound reason's rule,
He wonder'd she could play the fool.
She spoke with magic on her tongue,
While with a Syren's voice she sung;
Then touch'd the organ with such skill
That wound the Doctor to her will,
And by her flatt'ring power to please
So charm'd his sensibilities,

That he did all his views relate
To seek again the marriage state;
Nor did the dear Divine conceal
One awkward wish that he might feel.
—At once the frolic Madam caught
A plan with precious mischief fraught:
"O what an idle silly dance,"
She said, with warmth, "to trust to chance,
To hope by accident to find
A mate that's suited to your mind!
You've but a fortnight here to stay,
Scarce time to hear a *Yea* or *Nay*:
You can't to courtship's rules conform;
A siege won't do—attack by storm!"
Then she exclaim'd with tongue and eyes
"*We for a Wife will advertise!*"
She squeez'd his hand—and he complies.
"The happiest Hymen I e'er knew,"
She said, "from advertisements grew;
And to my friend, I wish it known
That I shall scarce except my own.
Nay do but trust the whole to me,
I am the soul of secrecy.
If this nice project should succeed,
You'll thank and bless me for the deed:
If it should fail, it is no more
Than wisdom's self has done before.
—Of candidates you need not fear;
Perhaps too many may appear;
But, ere their forms salute your eyes,
I'll learn their secret histories;
And you shall see, my rev'rend friend,
The one which I may recommend,
And if you think that one's the thing,
Then for the licence and the ring."

—The Doctor took it all for granted:
It seem'd as if he were enchanted.
Then, in impressive eloquence,
He spoke at once his grateful sense
Of her warm friendship and regard,
Though goodness is its own reward:
But both in mode as well as measure,
He left it all to her good pleasure.
—'Twas midnight past when he departed,
Charm'd with the plan and quite light-hearted,
Leaving his lady friend to dream
Of all the mischief of her scheme.

 Syntax now set his heart at rest,
Thought what was done was for the best,
And to fill up the interval
He would on dear Miss PALLET call.
Here his reception was most kind:
Sweet manners with superior mind,
And taste and genius were combin'd.
—When the first formal chat was o'er,
The works of Artists they explore,
Whose labours gain'd the height of fame
And fix'd the imperishable name.
They then the living talents try,
With just remark and critic eye.
"And now," she said, "you will incline
To tell me what you think of mine.
I hear you say, 'how sweet, how fine!'
But if, while your kind words commend,
You should see faults—O what a friend!"
"—I see no faults—but let me tell,
The leading power of painting well
Must spring from studying various nature
In ev'ry form and ev'ry feature:

'Tis that alone which can impart
The height and depth and breadth of art;
Nor do I see your pencil err
From that primeval character."
"Doctor," she said, "O will you stay
And take your dinner here to day:
You then will hear two Artists prate
Of Art—and who each other hate.
Such things there are—e'en lib'ral arts
Are known to poison human hearts,
And their warm feelings oft supply
With envy base and jealousy."
—The Artists came—" Sir, Mr. B——
'Tis Doctor Syntax: Mr. G——"
The dinner soon appear'd in view,
And pass'd as other dinners do:
But with the fruit the talk began,
And thus around the table ran.
—Said Syntax, "I my wonder own
Where a fair lady's art is shown,
That among all the figures here,
The God of Love does not appear."
"—We known professors of the art,"
Says G—— "have got him quite by heart:
We want no model, do you see,
Of this familiar Deity:
Sure am I, that I'm not so stupid,
But sleeping I could paint a Cupid."—
"—I wish you would the trouble take
To paint a Cupid when awake,"
Said titt'ring B—— "I know 'twill prove
A very sleepy God of Love."
"Have done! have done!" Miss Pallet said,
"The passion shall be well display'd,
Not as a Painter's eye may view it,
But as the Doctor's tongue can do it:—

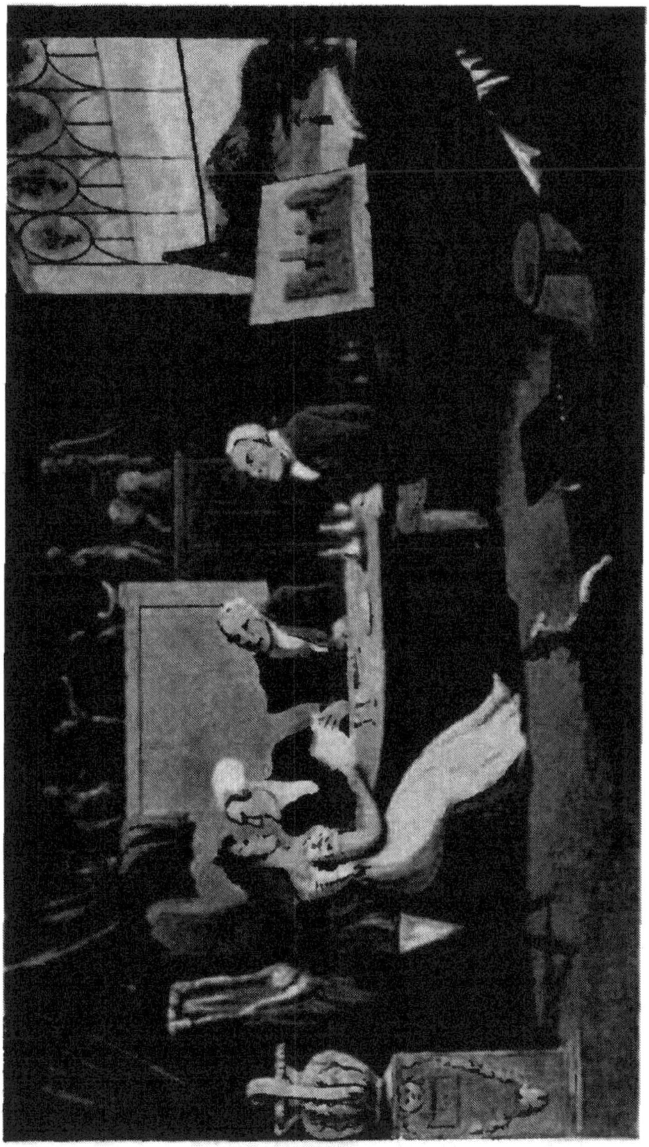

And therefore, Sirs, I humbly move
That he may speak his thoughts on Love."
"—'Tis a nice theme," Syntax replied,
"But ladies must not be denied:
Mine are peculiar thoughts I fear,
And I ask candour's self to hear.
—The passion that commands the heart
Is in this world *a thing apart*;
And throughout life, as we may learn,
Has nothing like a fix'd concern:
It makes fools wise, and wise men fools,
But not by any written rules.
Love, as recording Hist'ry shows,
Leads wisdom often by the nose:
Nature does female weakness arm
With that inexplicable charm
That oft without exterior grace,
Or piercing eye or lovely face,
Or e'en th' alluring power of wit,
Makes all-presuming man submit;
Assumes the full domestic reign,
And sees him smile to wear the chain.
It is a secret sympathy,
A hidden power that doth decree,
As in the world we often see,
Natures the most oppos'd to join
At the matrimonial shrine;
Nay, has been often known to match
Affection warm with hands that scratch;
And e'en in Hymen's net trepan,
The polish'd Peer and blowzy Nan.
Such the effect, but then the cause
Is work'd by Nature's hidden laws,
And if you ask me to explain
The *Whys* and *Wherefores*, 'tis in vain,
I cannot, and think no man can."

"—The Doctor knows the human heart,"
Says B—— "but can he talk of Art?"
"—That," says the Lady, "will appear:
If you will listen, you shall hear.
—What think you of this sketch, my friend?"
"In ev'ry part I do commend
Its force, its freedom," Syntax said:
When either Artist shook his head.
The Doctor then, in prudence clos'd
The observations he propos'd:
But thus continued:—"May I ask,
Should it be no unpleasant task,
To tell me, if the Arts abound
And flourish fair in British ground,
Where Science is so largely found?"
"—O no," 'twas said, "they're going down,
There's scarce an Artist of renown."
The Sage then mention'd many a name
That dwelt upon the lips of fame.
"O no," they said; then, one by one,
With many a shrug, they ran them down,
And only differ'd in degree,
As they let loose their calumny.
This colour'd not, that wanted vigour,
A third knew nothing of the figure:—
Thus having clos'd their critic law,
They Syntax ask'd if he could draw:
When he his ready pencil took
And in the blank page of a book,
Design'd a gallows, from which swung
Two figures that by cordage hung.
"Pray," it was said, "who may be those?
They are two murderers I suppose."
"Yes," Syntax said, "of my formation,
They're Murderers of Reputation."

—B—— a short time in silence sat,
Then slid away and took his hat :
The other sought the self-same track,
Nor said adieu, nor e'er came back.

"I think the lecture I have given,
Has not sent your good friends to Heaven,"
Syntax observ'd.   "No," 'twas replied,
"O what a lesson to their pride!
Which, if we could their feelings trace,
Has sent them to another place.—
—Though they have merit which is known,
They hate all merit but their own :
They cordially detest each other,
But both will join t'abuse another.
They're useful to me in my art,
And both lay claim to my poor heart :
But when they make their wishes known,
I laughing vow 'tis fled and gone :
Still they are faithless ; but to you,
I may declare that it is true ;
Though with calm patience I must wait
'Till the stars smile upon my fate.—
And now, dear Sir, I beg and pray,
Come often while in town you stay,
And be assur'd whene'er you come
To none but you I'll be at home!"

Syntax took leave with great delight,
In hopes to pass a tranquil night,
Without one unpropitious thought
Which a day's hurry might have brought :
But at his door attendant care,
In Pat's pale face, was waiting there.
With something like a wat'ry eye
Pat said, " I fear poor Punch will die.

I did not know where you were gone,
That I might ask what should be done;
But as I knew you would not spare
Expence to save the poor old mare,
I did the best assistance claim,
And Doctor Glanders quickly came:
I know not what he might discover,
But I am sure he gives her over.
Your Rev'rence—but to hear her moan,
And Oh!—so like a Christian groan,
Yes, it would melt a heart of stone."
"—My good friend Pat, what can I do?
The poor beast I must leave to you.
Go take your ale to soothe your sorrow,
And see me early on the morrow."
—Pat came to orders—op'd the door
And said, "poor Punch, Sir, is no more.
How oft have I the mare bestrode,
In field, through woods, and on the road!
Poor thing! she knew my voice as well
As the flock knows its leader's bell.
I've brush'd her grey skin o'er and o'er,
But I shall rub her down no more."
"—Now Pat, I pray you, hold your peace,"
The Doctor said, "your wailing cease:
I'm sorry that I've lost the mare,
But 'tis a loss which I can bear:
It is not worth this mighty pother;
She's gone, and we must get another:
Yet I will, for old Punch's sake,
Go and all due enquiry make,
And hear the stable-people state,
What caus'd her unexpected fate."
Syntax arriv'd when Glanders there
Was looking at the breathless mare:

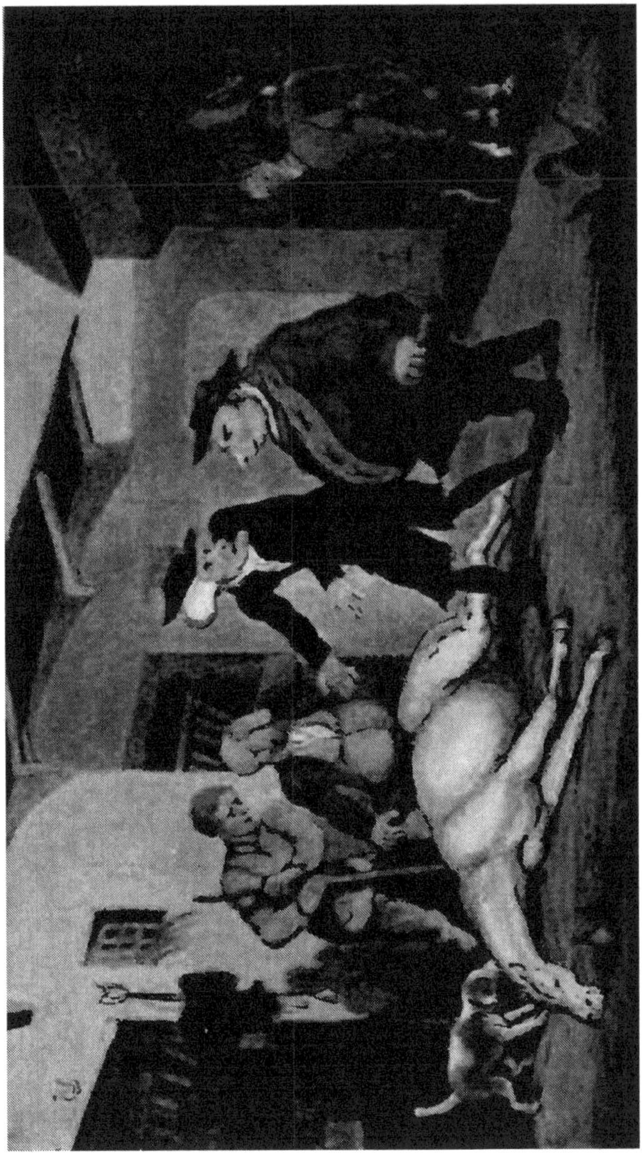

And soon an angry conflict rose,
Big with hard words that threaten'd blows.—
"What caus'd her death, Sir?" ask'd the Sage,
"Hard work," old Glanders said, "and age."
    S. "What do you think I'm such a Turk,
To kill the mare by over-work,
Who did, I say, for years conduce
Both to my pleasure and my use?
Whate'er my many faults may be,
I ne'er fail'd in humanity;
This my whole life I trust will show,
And all who long have known me know.
Nay, from your looks, it is a chance,
But she died from your ignorance."
    G. "Four hundred miles, though travell'd slow
At her old age, you must allow
Is hardish work,—What say you now?
I tell you too, I drew my knowledge
From the Veterinary College.
John Ostler there, I pray appear,
You know, at least, for many a year
I with success have practis'd here.
Again I say and you may stare,
It was hard work that kill'd your mare."
"—Oh! Oh!" cried Pat, "how my hand
    itches,
Thou guinea pig, in boots, and breeches,
To trounce thee well!—Thou lying sinner,
To beat thee I would lose my dinner!"
—Glanders deign'd not to make reply,
But, with grave look and leering eye,
Just utter'd: "Here is my account,
And I now beg the small amount."
Syntax began to fume and vapour,
And tore at once the dirty paper,

Within the house his voice was heard,
When the yard's master soon appear'd,
And did in humblest terms request
The Doctor's rage might be supprest.
"Though of strange form and uncouth feature,
Old Glanders is a useful creature:
And though his ways are coarse and rude,
He is with ample skill endued,
And is pursued by hourly calls
For all the ails of animals;
Nay, does his ready aid supply,
From sporting stable to the sty.
Indeed, I think, if skill or care
Could have preserv'd your old grey mare,
She would not have been lying there.
Leave, Sir, this bus'ness all to me,
It is beneath your dignity;
And, if another horse you buy,
My judgment shall its aid supply."
—Smiles and kind words, how great their skill,
To regulate the wayward will!
And, in this out-of-humour hour,
Syntax was soften'd by their power.
"Thank you," he said, "my honest friend,
To your good counsel I attend."
Then spoke, as round his eyes he threw,
"Pat come with me!—Poor Punch, adieu!"

"An' please you, I ne'er long'd," says Pat,
"Since my round head has worn a hat,
T' employ my fists as on that fellow,
That half-grown, o'er-grown Punchinello!"
Said Syntax, "prithee hold thy tongue:
I fear that we have both been wrong;
And, when we do our errors find,
'Tis well to give them to the wind,

And with more care our way pursue
In what we yet may have to do.

   Good, rev'rend man, with all thy knowledge,
First gain'd at school, enlarg'd at college,
And by hard study still improv'd
In the long track where thought has mov'd;
With thy strict honour, gen'rous worth,
And all those virtues which have birth
In the warm, unpolluted heart,
Where cunning low or tutor'd art
Was never, never known to dwell,
Whence all who know thee love thee well;
With piety that from above
Has caught the flame of sacred love,
That, not confin'd to time or place,
Extends to all the human race;
With all that thou hast known and seen
In the wide space that lies between
The time when on the chin appears
Manhood'd first down and fifty years;
With that shrewd and sagacious mind
That can the depths of learning find,
And with the critic eye explore
The dubious paths of ancient lore,
Draw hidden knowledge from the night
Of ages past, and give it light—
With this and all your boasted care,
You see not the insidious snare
That female frolic does prepare,
Not to seek vice within its bower,
For that is not within her power,
Nor, to say truth, does her design
To such dark malice e'er incline;
But 'tis to make you play the fool,
To be the sport of ridicule,

To make you in the mischief chime,
As buffoon in the pantomime,
And hold your fancies up to view
T' amuse her half-bred, giggling crew,
In such a way, and such a place,
As might be bordering on disgrace.—
—It almost makes me melancholy,
To think my pen must tell your folly;
But still I can with safety say,
When you, my friend, from wisdom stray,
It is your virtues that betray,
Or failings which, to good allied,
Are fighting seen by virtue's side.
Such are the sources, I well know,
From which your venial errors flow;
But with them all, I wish most true,
That I were half as good as you.
—For how can the mind's eye see clear,
When vanity presents the ear?
How can suspicion close the heart,
When grateful thoughts their warmth impart?
How can it fond belief deny,
When urg'd by sensibility?
How turn away and not attend,
When beauty says, I am your friend?
And when it adds, my friendship use,
Can the kind spirit then refuse?—
—But I cease to apostrophise
The unthought frailties of the wise;
And, my kind friends, shall lay before ye
The future progress of my story.

 The Doctor now employ'd his pen,
In letters kind to Sommerden:
With feelings rather grave than gay
He pass'd a sentimental day;

Though a late evening hour was cheer'd,
When Vellum's smiling face appear'd.
They smok'd their pipes and chatted o'er
The topics of the passing hour.
At length 'twas said; "I here have brought,
As matter for your future thought,
A written paper that contains
What I propose as mutual gains,
Which will, as you may plainly see,
Transfer your manuscript to me."
Syntax the paper keenly ey'd,
And thus without reserve replied:
"I own your very liberal feelings,
My friend, in all our former dealings,
And I'm content, I must avow,
With what you're pleas'd to offer now;
And when I throw into account
Your kindness, with its full amount,
What I expected to receive
Is less than you propose to give."
—The solemn contract thus agreed,
Without delay in word and deed,
Old Vellum, when away he went,
Left Syntax, like himself, content.
—The literary business done,
And the pleas'd Doctor now alone,
On what was pass'd in accents grave
His candour thus its judgment gave.
"—He acted with a tradesman's care,
But all I've seen was right and fair,
And I in justice must commend
His conduct as a civil friend;
And should I hear abuse of Vellum,
I would in strong expressions tell 'em
This reputable man of letters
Is just and gen'rous as his betters."

Next morning as he calmly took
His coffee, poring o'er a book,
A letter from Ma'am Briskit came,
That did his quick attention claim.
He broke the seal, then rubb'd his head,
And thus aloud the epistle read :—

"*Try, My Dear Doctor, all your art,*
To make yourself supremely smart,
For ere 'tis mid-day you will see
Two pleasing objects, I think three,
To claim your fond idolatry.
But then they will not come alone,
Each has a friend to make her known,
Because, to speak their several state
Must shock you as indelicate.
A kind aunt will on one attend,
Another has a guardian friend,
And with the youngest of the three,
You will a tender mother see.
Either of them will suit you well ;
I've seen them all, and all excel
In diff'rent ways perhaps, but still,
If in my sex I've any skill,
They must your utmost wish fulfil :
Your heart, of course will fix on one,
And then the important deed is done.
I've been to my commission true,
And so, my dear Divine, Adieu !
While I possess the power to frisk it,
I shall be yours,
                        Susanna Briskit."

The Doctor conn'd the letter o'er,
And thoughts arose unthought before :

IN SEARCH OF A WIFE

Nay strange suspicions now began
To seize upon the inner man;
And ere he could arrange his view
Of what it now were best to do,
About the door a certain stir
Announc'd a two-fold visitor.
The elder said, " Sir, if you please,
Permit me to present my niece."
But the prim lady scarce had spoke,
When, in a voice like raven's croak,
Another said, "I here attend,
As counsellor to this my friend,
Who for your sake would feel a pride
In laying widow's weeds aside."
Another at that moment came,
A somewhat of a dashing dame:
" My daughter, Sir, I here present,
The excess of all accomplishment."
—Syntax observing on each face
A certain smother of grimace,
" Pat, I command you keep the door,
Nor entrance give to any more,"
He then exclaim'd, "and now I pray,
What, ladies fair, have you to say?"
—In a strange kind of bustling fuss,
They in succession answer'd thus:
"—I am first cousin to a Lord,
And therefore claim your earliest word."
"My niece is of superior age,
And should the first your ear engage."
'—My child is youngest of the three,
As at a glance, Sir, you may see,
And if you 'bide by Love's decorum,
She, Doctor, should be heard before 'em."
"—Ladies," he said, "I plainly see
The tricks that you would play with me.

In all that's said, in all that's done,
I see 'tis Mistress Briskit's fun;
I feel I am a very fool,
And well deserve your ridicule;
But if you do not quickly go,
A Constable the way shall show."
"—Was ever any thing so rude!
Was ever such ingratitude!"
About the room their tongues resounded:
And 'twas confusion worse confounded.
"We came not here for nought you know,
And we will kiss you ere we go;
For though we do not gain our ends,
Pray, sweet Sir, let us part as friends,
We only claim what is our due,
And each expects a kiss from you."
—The Doctor did defence prepare,
And barricadoed with a chair,
But what, alas, was to be done,
'Twas fearful odds, 'twas six to one.
Thus they the angry Sage assail'd,
He kick'd and fought, but they prevail'd.
Urg'd by his passion as by shame,
Thus loudly did the Sage exclaim:
"Pat, turn these beldames out I pray,
O make them, make them brush away,
By any means, or smooth or rough,
I care not how you get them off."
Says Pat, "I hear, Sir, your commands,
I'll take the ladies off your hands!
And now I beg, my pretty dears,
That you will lay aside your fears;
I'll do your ladyship no harm,
I'll kiss you well, and make you warm.
So come along my sweetest honeys,
For love like mine hates ceremonies."

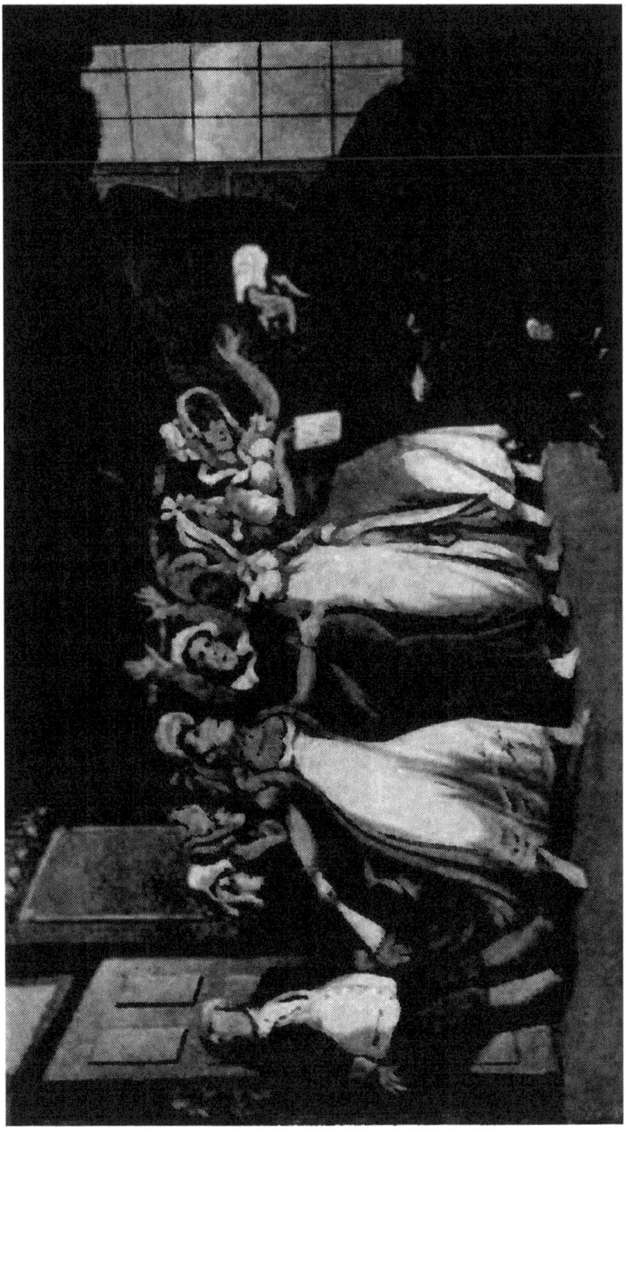

He kept his word with no small bustling,
Muslins were torn, and silks were rustling,
And as they glided tow'rds the stair,
He smack'd and clapp'd each passing fair,
But the muse must not mention where.
—Pat, who was now in all his glory
Thus hurried onward with his story.
" Sir, as the party went down stairs
With frowning looks and humbled airs,
And halted on the landing-places,
To brush up their disorder'd graces,
I bid them send their Mrs. Briskit
Just to visit us and frisk it,
As we had a rod in pickling,
To give her fancy such a tickling,
That with all her fine pretences,
Would soon restore her to her senses.
Something of this kind she will play,
As her maids told me, ev'ry day.
Nay, would you think, Sir, this sweet jewel,
Once drove her husband to a duel;
Who stood a shot to make amends
For her mad fits of odds and ends!"
"—All's well that ends well, honest Pat,
So we will think no more of that,"
The Doctor said, and, tir'd of riot,
He sought the sofa's lulling quiet,
Resign'd to sleep's oblivious power,
'Till time announc'd the dinner hour.

It may have been before observ'd,
The Doctor's stomach never swerv'd
From all those duties, morn or night,
Which wait on genuine appetite;
His spirits therefore now had gain'd
The strength by dainty food attain'd;

And as he did the goblet quaff,
He found himself dispos'd to laugh,
And not to think with fretful spleen
At the past morning's senseless scene,
Though with self-taunting ridicule,
He would just call himself a fool.
This evening he was quite alone,
Patrick and Mrs. Broom were gone,
And, as he pac'd the chamber floor,
His journey past he ponder'd o'er:
And though his hopes it did not crown,
Yet many pleasures, he must own,
He had in its long circuit known;
Mix'd up indeed with various whim,
That was familiar quite to him.
For he still felt the Quixote spirit,
Which he was destin'd to inherit
From his long-past, e'en boyish age,
To that which now had dubb'd him sage.
—He had his little business done,
And it was time he should be gone:
Still he another week would stay,
And for his mere amusement stray
About this wond'rous town, to see
What wakens curiosity.
Nor was this all, poor Punch had died,
Her vacant stall must be supplied;
And, now his mind was more at ease,
On the fair Artist's power to please
He dwelt, and on the ample measure
She could dispense of solid pleasure,
So that he did, at least, refer
A day to reason and to her.
—Thus as he turned his projects o'er,
A rap resounded at the door.

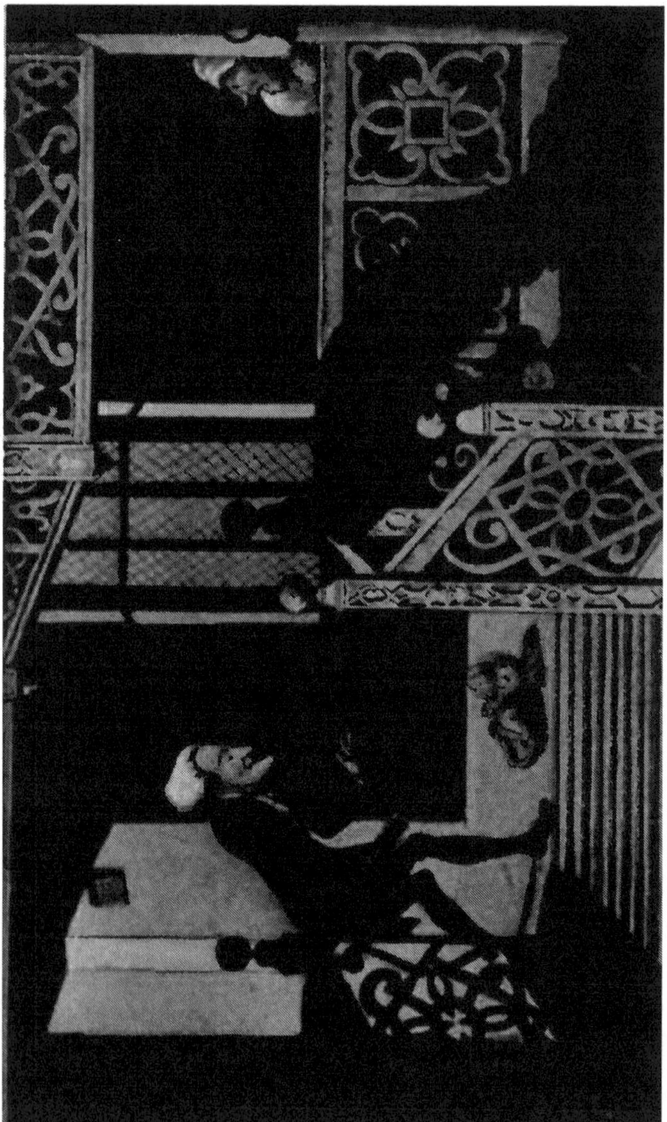

"Well! Well!" he thought, "what can this be,
To break in on my reverie?
Old Vellum ne'er so late would come,
As 'tis his time for gadding home."
He op'd the door, and 'gan to stare,
For lo, no visitor was there;
But, looking onward to the floor,
There was a basket cover'd o'er
With a warm blanket, which remov'd,
The covering of an infant prov'd:
There a sweet, lovely baby slept,
And look'd as if it ne'er had wept.
Syntax, now all amazement, said,
Or rather lift his hands and pray'd:
"O save me, Heaven, what shall I do?"
Exclaiming, on a closer view,
"And Heaven I trust will save thee too!"
A neighbouring Lawyer op'd his door,
The exclamation to explore,
When Syntax, all amazement, said,
"Here at my door a child is laid."
"Well," the Attorney then replied,
"By no law is it specified
That you're oblig'd to take it in."
"But think," said Syntax, "what a sin
To leave the infant here to lie
Throughout the night—perhaps to die!
It would be murder in my creed,
And my heart shudders at the deed."
The Lawyer then withdrew his light,
Said, "Wish you joy, and so good night."
—A message soon reach'd Mrs. Broom,
With orders instantly to come.
Short was her period of complying,
For she thought Syntax must be dying;

But when she came and found him well,
How she began her joy to tell.
" But then, Sir, why this mighty hurry?
I really am in such a flurry!"
" It is the same," he said, "with me,
Beneath that cloth the cause you'll see."
And then he told the history.
"O," she exclaim'd, "the wretched creature,
That thus could violate her nature!
Indeed Sir, it may not be civil,
But such a mother is a devil!"
"Good Mrs. Broom, that may be true,
But say what are we now to do,
For we must instantly prepare
To make this innocent our care."
"O 'tis a charming babe," she said,
" As ever was in cradle laid.
O such a cherub to destroy—
But is it, Sir, a girl or boy?"
The Sage replied, "pray look and see,
For that is yet unknown to me."
She on her nose the glasses plac'd,
And the sweet, sleeping figure trac'd;
"O," she exclaim'd, " the truth I scan;
When he grows up he'll be a man!
'Tis well, Sir, that it is no worse,
For I now know a ready nurse,
And ere that you are gone to rest
The babe shall find a milky breast."
The Doctor then the foundling eyed,
And thus in soften'd tones replied:
"Let the same tender love be shown
As if the infant were my own:
I leave the creature to thy care,
Nor cost nor fondest caution spare."

IN SEARCH OF A WIFE

He kiss'd the infant as it went,
Then smil'd, for goodness beam'd content.
—'Twas a droll day, few such we see,
But such the Doctor's destiny.
At morn, three would-be wives besought him;
At night a new-born child was brought him:
But these strange haps did not molest
The tranquil temper of his breast;
Nor did it cause a wakeful eye,
When the slow, midnight hour drew nigh.
—Sweet are the slumbers of the good,
And Syntax slept as virtue should.

The morning came and Pat appear'd,
Full of the story he had heard,
With feelings of parental care
But still of anger no small share
'Gainst those that brought the infant there.
He did not fear the child would perish,
He knew there was a heart to cherish,
Nor ever to the parish send it,
But where 'twas left would there befriend it.
—At length there with the laundress came
An humble, curtsying, comely dame,
Of pleasing aspect, neatly dress'd,
With the poor foundling at her breast,
Where active instinct seem'd to cling
As if it were its native spring.
"Last week," she said, " I lost my own,
And I will nurse this little one
With all the fond and tender care
As if my child were milking there.
Who knows, good Sir, but on my word,
I think its sire may be a Lord.

Dear heart, the linen is so fine,
And work'd with such a nice design,
Nay, here and there, with flow'rs beset,
My fancy sees a Coronet!"
"Heaven," said the Doctor, "only knows
To whom the babe existence owes;
But this I know, and will not spare,
To whom it owes a parent's care:
Therefore, good woman, I commend
Its wants to you, and pray attend,
As if th' unconscious infant had
Some rake of title for it's dad,
Who for your service paid you well,
That you might not the secret tell.
I have no other anxious wish,
But from the full and flowing dish
Which nature gives you, it may share
Its wonted meal, with ev'ry care,
'Till the due weaning hour demands
Encreas'd attention at your hands;
When I shall leave a faithful friend
Who to your counsel will attend,
And whose kind power is well prepar'd
To satisfy and to reward.
For, while I live, the life that Heaven
Has thus to my protection given
Shall want no necessary care
That Christian duty bids prepare."
The nurse each promise kind profess'd,
And clasp'd the infant to her breast;
While Mrs. Broom, with fond surprise,
Applied her apron to her eyes.
The good folks wept and then they smil'd,
Bless'd the good deed and kiss'd the child;
Nor took their leaves with signs of sorrow,
When told to bring him there to-morrow.

IN SEARCH OF A WIFE

Syntax, who felt his tutor'd heart
Was doubly fitted to impart
Those higher feelings which bestow
The wish to lessen human woe,
Or do their active powers employ
To aid the flow of human joy,
Bade his thoughts range that they might find
A spot just suited to his mind ;
If not, to pass the day alone
Was a resource to him well known.
But 'twas not long ere reason's voice,
With pleasure join'd, declar'd the choice.
Miss PALLET's study was the place
Where he should find a smiling face,
Which would with brighten'd eye declare
An unaffected welcome there.
—He went, she saw, and rang the bell,
When she was heard aloud to tell
Th' attendant maid, "let who will come,
Remember I am not at home.
'Tis a vain moment I allow,"
She added, "but I would bestow
If such a phrase I dare avow,
A day upon my learned friend,
Which his warm favour may commend,
And in his kind remembrance shine,
As it will ever do in mine."
—Here the delighted Doctor sat
In grave debate or lively chat,
With no vain folly to deride him,
But with attention's ear beside him
And such a mind, where he could pour
His sage instructions, treasur'd lore ;
Nay, whence 'twould be return'd again
In accents soft and humble strain.

At length fish, ham and roasted chicken,
With peas and tart, form'd pretty picking:
Nor was there wanting port or sherry,
Which would have made him more than merry,
If he had wanted mode or measure
To aid his sense of present pleasure.
Miss too from Pat contriv'd to glean
That, to complete the social scene,
A pipe the afternoon would bless
With unexpected happiness:
And when she did the tube command,
He bent the knee and kiss'd the hand
That did the cherish'd gift present,
Which gave perfection to content.
—Such was the sentimental duet;
With pleasure does my fancy view it:
The wise, the kind instructor he,
The pleas'd, attentive list'ner she;
Receiving all his words pursued
With beaming smiles of gratitude.
She was a fine, accomplish'd creature,
A student of those powers of nature,
That clothe the earth and charm the eye
With ravishing variety:
And though with sister arts endow'd,
She was too virtuous to be proud,
But kept the course we seldom see,
From ev'ry vain pretension free,
And grac'd with calm humility.
They talk'd of arts—the room around
Did with fine specimens abound;
And e'en the window open'd wide
On rising hills and flowing tide,
Which her fine pencil gave to hide
An old, beplaster'd dismal wall
That cross'd th' opposing interval.

—Her beauty was a certain grace
That play'd about her air and face,
And a mark'd unassuming sense
Was cloth'd with artless eloquence:
While his Quixotic praise enshrin'd
The embellish'd pictures of her mind.
Nor did they thoughts on Love deny,
When the fair Artist heav'd a sigh,
Though she ne'er ventur'd to explain
The cause of her resistless pain:
She only said she must endure it,
And that hope told her time would cure it.
E'en by her silence it was shown
That her fond heart was not her own.
So that if he did then incline
To say, "I wish thou wouldst be mine,"
He saw and heard enough to prove,
'Twas not for him to offer love.

With Syntax and his *Idol mio*
Who would not wish to form a *trio!*
When, sometimes grave and sometimes gay,
The lengthen'd evening pass'd away.
—The Doctor was forewarn'd by pride
Ma'am Briskit's impudence to hide,
And, therefore, he made nothing known
Of folly he had blush'd to own;
But with a tear and half a smile
That did his feelings reconcile,
He told the foundling's curious lot,
And what a present he had got.
By some it would be thought distressing,
But he—that it would prove a blessing—
A blessing where a power was given
T' obey the first command of Heaven,

And like th' Egyptian princess, save
An outcast infant from the grave.
"Yes, yes," he said, "it shall receive
Each fond attention I can give,
And 'till a parent comes to claim
The rights of a parental name,
I will my sense of duty prove,
Nor shall it want a parent's love:
And if, my dear, and charming friend
You to its state would condescend,
If your blest charity would share, ⎫
Or watch, at least, the nurse's care, ⎬
'Till it grows into strength to bear ⎭
A journey to my tranquil home,
Where you, I trust, will one day come,
I will before Heaven's altar plead,
To bless you for the virtuous deed!"
"Fear not," she said, with moisten'd eye,
"My friendship or my charity;
And, when the spring's returning hours,
Shall clothe with green your peaceful bowers,
The babe in all its cherish'd charms
Shall fill its foster-father's arms."
—The time now came when they must part
With mutual wishes of the heart.
The fair-one, with a modest grace,
Receiv'd the Doctor's kind embrace,
With promise to embrace again,
Ere he set off for SOMMERDEN.

Next morn he ask'd the child to see,
And all was as it ought to be:
But, as the time was drawing on
When he had settled to be gone,

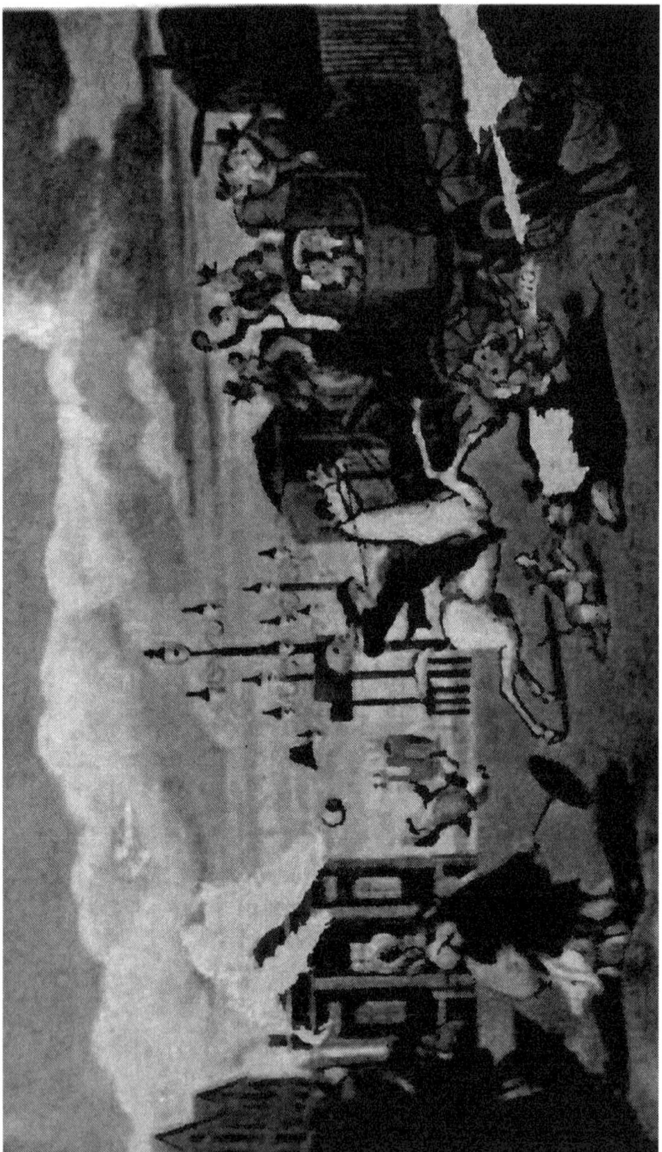

It now became his anxious care
The loss unlook'd for to repair
Of Punch, that dear, departed mare.
His breakfast paper told the tale,
At Hyde-Park-Corner, of a sale,
Where he 'ndulg'd the hope to find
A beast of burden to his mind.
Bays, chesnuts, blacks and greys were shown,
Or for the road, or field, or town,
And a stout mare he chanc'd to see,
Which seem'd to suit him to a T:
Nay, while he on the creature gaz'd,
He heard its ev'ry action prais'd
By certain busy jockey buyers,
Who look'd too honest to be liars.
He bade—the mare was soon his own,
The money paid, the bus'ness done,
And he in gay equestrian pride
Forth from the yard was seen to ride:
But soon his sad mistake was found;
He ne'er had ask'd if she were sound.
—What was the mischief of her nature,
Or what vagary seiz'd the creature;
What trick her hinder parts assail,
Or prickly branch to wound her tail,
Which stable frolic might impel,
Though I suspect, I cannot tell,
But she set off at such a rate
That, as she pass'd the turnpike gate,
The toll-man well nigh met his fate.
Away the hat and peruke flew,
A cabbage-merchant he o'erthrew;
And while the dame was sprawling laid,
Her angry donkey kick'd and bray'd:
Nay, nought could check the wild mare's rage
But running headlong 'gainst a stage,

Which caus'd a scene of strange distress,
That language knows not to express.
Half breathless and with naked pate
Syntax on his mad palfrey sat;
While she at length obey'd the reins,
Stopp'd by the shock which shook her brains.
The inner passengers alarm'd,
Scream'd from affright, though none were harm'd;
While from the dickey and the roof
Was heard the loud and coarse reproof,
Mix'd with loud laugh and scoffing groan,
As the unconscious coach drove on.
The Doctor, with astonish'd air,
Dismounted from the trembling mare,
And soon, alas, was taught to find
Th' unwelcome secret—she was blind!
'Tis well that, for the Doctor's cost,
No limb was broke, no life was lost,
And half-a-score of shillings paid
For all the tricks that had been play'd,
The wand'ring hat and wig were sought,
Which on a poor sweep's head were brought;
Who met them on his road to town,
And proudly wore them as his own.
—Just in the midst of this disaster,
Pat had now haply reach'd his master.
And, with the sightless mare, they sought
The place where she had just been bought;
When Syntax loudly 'gan to preach
Or rather to let forth a speech,
When he so talk'd of rogues and cheating,
That certain horsewhips threaten'd beating:
But Pat stood forth and boldly vow'd,
Whoever such an insult show'd
Should ne'er again speak out a threat,
Or lift an angry hand to beat,

Wielding a pretty piece of wood
That would have made his promise good.
But as he still continued railing
And in harsh terms the place assailing,
Nay, did in venom'd language strike
Buyers and sellers all alike,
The Doctor might have found disgrace
Among the sharp-set jockey race;
But so it was, a friend was nigh
To calm his rash perplexity—
The kind and friendly Baronet,
Whom he some years ago had met
In his first journey to the North,
And known for opulence and worth,
Who, shaking Syntax by the hand,
Could scarce a bursting laugh command,
Thinking to what a market he
Had brought his learn'd philosophy,
And in his Greek and Latin trade
What a blind purchase he had made.
"My wonder there is no concealing,"
The Knight exclaim'd, "to find you dealing
In this far-fam'd equestrian college,
Where all your stores of various knowledge
Would be as useless as the stone
Which you now chance to stand upon.
But now, my friend, take no more care
About this awkward, strange affair.
I am a Yorkshireman, and breed
For this same market many a steed,
And I, my rev'rend friend, will see
Into this same rascality:
I will take care that you shall find
The bus'ness settled to your mind.
I therefore counsel you to pop
Your head in some Bookseller's shop,

And there your vacant time amuse
'Till four, with chit-chat or the news;
Then for my dinner pray prepare,
On the south-side of Portman-Square,
And let your servant too be there."
"Thank you, good Sir, and I obey,"
Was all the Doctor had to say.
Suffice it, at the hour of four,
Sir John receiv'd him at his door,
With "your foul, ugly matter's o'er.
I've swapp'd your grey mare for a bay,
And you have not a doit to pay:
A useful, handsome, trav'lling hack,
As e'er had Doctor on its back;
And if your sturdy valet's come,
He may now mount and take her home."
Orders were given, and smiling Pat,
With many a doffing of his hat,
Was quickly seen with sprightly air
Trotting the purchase 'cross the square.

Syntax, with all that powerful feeling
Which good hearts catch from gen'rous dealing,
Said little, rather he said nought;
His mind, involv'd in grateful thought,
Check'd the quick impulse of his tongue,
'Till, dinner o'er, the glasses rung;
When Burgundy and brisk Champagne
Awoke the gay, convivial strain.
The Doctor told his hist'ry o'er,
Sir John delighted wish'd for more,
And Time, as it was growing late,
Broke up at length the tête-à-tête.
But ere the well-fed Doctor went,
Contented he, his host content,

The latter did his wishes tell
Before he said, good-night, farewell!
"You say, that ere three days are past
You tow'rds your northern home must haste;
Now let me tell you, ere a day
Is clos'd, as you pursue your way,
You will a stately mansion see,
Where you must stop and ask for me.
There dwells a noble Lord, whose worth
Equals your patron's in the North,
And as a truth I'm pleas'd to tell,
Whom I admire and love as well.
In him the image you will see
Of noble hospitality;·
By whom your worth will be discern'd
And learning known, for he is learn'd.
To-morrow I this place shall seek,
Where I prepare to pass a week,
And you will do yourself much wrong,
If you remain not there as long;
Nay, I myself will smooth the way,
Or for your short or longer stay."
—Syntax, revolving in his mind
Honour and luxury combin'd,
And where his dazzled eyes would see
Life, in its rich embroidery,
Express'd in a most joyous measure
Both his obedience and his pleasure.
—He took his leave—the hour was late,
As he return'd through Gray's-Inn-Gate,
When he found Pat his vigils keeping,
In snoring and most soundly sleeping,
Who, after many a hurried shake
That did th' o'erpow'ring stupor wake,
Would in exulting tones declare
The virtues of the purchas'd mare,

Whom all announc'd as safe and sound,
And must have cost full three-score pound.
This and much more:—"Have done! have done!"
Syntax exclaim'd, "the clock strikes one!"
When, with the day's fatigue opprest,
His bed he sought and sunk to rest.

   The morrow was a busy day:
For his departure no delay
Th' impatient Doctor would admit:
London he now resolv'd to quit;
Nay, thought it could not be too soon,
Why not that very afternoon?
To Pat he made his wishes known,
With orders that all might be done,
To quicken the departing hour
Which would commence his homeward tour.
But Pat just hinted they must stay
For packing due another day,
As the soil'd linen was just sent
To wash-tub's cleansing management,
And certain clothes, from rents and tears,
Were at the taylor's for repairs.
Now, as th' unwelcome truths he told,
The room-door open'd and behold
Good Mrs. Broom—when with her came
The smirking, curtsying, comely dame,
Who, smiling on the foundling's charms,
Would place it in the Doctor's arms.
He, half-afraid and half-asham'd,
Refus'd the boon, when she exclaim'd,
"You need not fear, depend upon't
You've held five hundred at the font,
And do not, Sir, look grave and frown,
I'm sure you'll love it as your own."

It was not that his heart relented
Or of his charity repented;
But that he saw another cause
In present haste to make a pause
That a whole day might be beguil'd
In some provision for the child.
At length, howe'er, the babe he kiss'd,
And when he had the charge dismiss'd,
He told the laundress to apply
To the parochial ministry,
That ev'ry sacred rite be done,
And the poor child be christen'd JOHN.
He order'd too, that twice each week,
The nurse would dear Miss Pallet seek,
Who would o'er all his wants preside,
As a kind patroness and guide.
" But let me ask, for, in this town,"
The Doctor said, " strange things are done,
How shall I know, when, brought to me,
It is the self-same child I see;
And that the foundling does not come
A changeling to my distant home!"
"Fear not," she answer'd, " I will show
A sign by which the child you'll know:
It is not in the baby's face,
Nor do I chuse to name the place:
A *Strawberry*, as blushing red
As when it ripens on its bed,
Does on a certain part appear,
Though I, Sir, must not tell you where;
Nay, it is such a curious mark,
That you may feel it in the dark.
The mother, when encreas'd in waist,
Long'd I suppose the fruit to taste,

And, as her wish was not obtain'd,
Th' unconscious child this mark has gain'd.
—When I was big, Sir, with my Stephen,
Who now is singing hymns in Heaven,
I long'd for *Pork*—I'm not mistaken,
And the dear child was mark'd with *Bacon*:
Nay, at the time when beans were ripe
It grew more like its prototype,
And never fail'd to meet the eye
In vegetating sympathy.
The mother's longing makes it so
As Doctors say—and they should know."

The Sage, who was his coffee taking,
Laugh'd 'till his very sides were shaking;
And, waken'd to a lively key,
By Goody Broom's philosophy,
He lost at once his teasing sense
Of hurry and impatience,
And thus determin'd to delay
His journey to another day;
And with Miss Pallet to enjoy,
Without allay, without alloy,
The hours that might remain his own
Ere he forsook the smoky town.
To her his willing steps he bent,
And as her list'ning ear she lent,
He told his plans, unveil'd his cares,
Display'd what were his hopes and fears,
His purpose ne'er again to roam
From his lake-side and pleasant home;
Nor more indulge in fancy's dream,
Nor let the air-built flatt'ring scheme
Of worldly interest turn aside
His mind from reason as its guide;

But while th' allotted moments pass,
As the sands lessen in the glass,
By duty's ordinance to move
In the strait path of social love;
T'enjoy the various good that's given,
To seek and teach the way to heaven,
And cheerful view the curtain fall—
The common fate that waits us all.

   I do not mean to reason, why
('Tis not in my philosophy)
A dainty dinner meal inherits
The power to elevate the spirits;
But this I know, that Syntax never
Appear'd so lively or so clever,
As when he found superior work
For the display of knife and fork:
Thus when the Lady's dinner came,
The mild and sentimental flame
By lively sallies was suppress'd
And yielded to the active zest
Which, at the table and long after,
Made dear Miss Pallet burst with laughter.
But, as the time drew nigh to part,
More solemn thoughts resum'd his heart,
And the fair Artist thus combin'd
The sense of her reflecting mind.
"—Your high renown, dear Sir, for learning,
Is far beyond my weak discerning;
But still I surely may aspire
To feel as well as to admire
The eloquence and brilliant wit
That does each rising object fit;
And humour that ne'er passes by
The offer'd opportunity.

Yet I must own, that I prefer
The dignity of character,
Which, leaving frolic out of sight,
Does the mind's higher taste delight;
The nobler sense which virtue loves,
And while it pleasure gives improves;
Becalms the pressing sense of pain,
When fun plays all its tricks in vain:
Nay, e'en in sorrow's mournful hour,
It offers its consoling power;
And though tears glisten in the eyes,
The heart in smiles will sympathise.
—The tale that does our feelings soften
Cannot be heard or read too often;
But laughing tricks, however treated,
Are stupid always when repeated:
When novelty no more supplies
The quick sensation of surprise,
The joke grows dull nor will beguile
The forewarn'd list'ner e'en to smile.
The proverb says, there's nought so stale,
So stupid as a twice told tale.
Unless it has a higher bent,
When rais'd and gemm'd by sentiment,
Then 'twill repeated pleasure give,
While the heart melts and virtues live:
And you ne'er please my mind so much,
As when on those high points you touch
Which the soul's brighter flights display
That bear me from myself away.
But you command the two-fold power:
The solemn and the lively hour
Alike, in pleasing change, submit
Or to your wisdom or your wit;
And, with rare energies combin'd,
You rule the muscles and the mind.

Within the hour that's passing by ⎫
My heart has felt a heav'nly sigh, ⎬
And laughter moisten'd either eye: ⎭
But though my higher feelings bend
To the grave maxims you commend,
Believe me, I am nothing loth
In season due to feel them both."

This and much more the Doctor heard,
When he his foundling's suit preferr'd,
And as he urg'd her heart to move
With pitying and protecting love,
She said her utmost to content him
About the child whom Heaven had sent
    him,
And to repay her gen'rous care,
Ask'd but his blessing and his prayer.
That blessing from his heart was given,
And his prayer crav'd the grace of Heaven:
For well he knew that pious prayer
Is sure to find admission there:
And he had learn'd the happy way,
Both how to bless and how to pray.
—A warm embrace, a fond adieu,
Clos'd this kind-hearted interview,
With hopes of time so charming, when
They both should meet at SOMMERDEN.

The morning of the following day
Did by its hurrying scene betray
His wild impatience to be gone
From this ungenial, smoky town.
Once more he saw the foundling press'd
To the fond nurse's welcome breast,

And view'd with scrutinizing eye
The spot mark'd by the *Strawberry*.

 His bills were then cast up and paid,
And gen'rous presents duly made,
When Mrs. Broom, with added zeal,
Prepar'd once more his dainty meal:
Thus did he in contentment dine,
And cocker'd up with hope and wine,
He felt the evening, as the last,
Must be with friendly Vellum past.
Nor did the Doctor fail to go
To the bright region of the Row;
There tiff'd his punch and talk'd and smok'd,
Was sometimes grave and sometimes jok'd;
But when he ventur'd to explore
Th' adventure at the chamber door,
And 'gan to tell the curious tale,
Vellum cried hush! and, like a snail,
Mov'd slowly onward, as in search
Of some one waiting in the lurch.
At length he said, "It is most true,
The secret I may tell to you,
I wish'd to keep my wife in view:
I sought with caution to find out
What my good woman was about;
For, I believe, in human nature,
There ne'er was such a curious creature,
So fond to place a list'ning ear
Where'er she may a secret hear:
But as a meagrim in her head
Has sent her to an early bed,
You may, my Rev'rend Sir, proceed,
And tell of this irrev'rent deed."
—Syntax proceeded to unveil
The strange and unexpected tale,

Nor, from false shame or awkward pride,
Did he his real feelings hide:
Nay, told, with an expressive eye,
Where last he saw a *Strawberry*.
"—Mercy," said Vellum, "if my dear
Had caught a tithe of what I hear,
O what a blessed curtain lecture
Might my foreboding fears conjecture!
She would, by jealousy beguil'd,
Have made me father of the child,
And sworn that you, to hide my sin,
Had ta'en th' adult'rous bantling in.
You hear Paul's clock now striking ten,
And 'till that hour is struck again,
When the grave bus'ness of the day
Must call me from her tongue away,
She would not those revilings cease
Which interrupt domestic peace,
And ev'ry child she heard or view'd
Would have the painful scene renew'd.
She also might, to aid her jeers,
Have beat my wig about my ears,
For 'tis, to you the truth I own,
No more than what her hand has done;
Nay, from the pillows, 'tis most certain,
I've oft been shelter'd by the curtain.
Doctor, that matrimonial ring
I've found a very serious thing!
And should Poll be the first to die,
Should that be Heav'n's kind destiny,
That ring she in her shroud shall wear,
Nor will I e'er the loss repair:
Nay, when this symbol death shall smother,
I swear I ne'er will buy another.
—If you had said, to save my bacon,
Dear Madam, you are quite mistaken,

You're not to Vellum's virtue just,
And wrongfully his love mistrust,
As I explain the facts to you,
The story's literally true;
Had you said this and even more
Her tranquil spirit to restore,
You would have heard this warm reply,
'Doctor! I tell you, Sir, YOU LIE!'
—Not all the water in the streams
That swell the flow of silver Thames,
No, nor the Thames, in all its pride,
When heighten'd by the Ocean's tide,
No, nor all the power of reason,
Would cleanse me from the fancied treason."
—Syntax did not the subject press,
But smil'd and wish'd him all success
In ev'ry scheme of passing life,
That might embrace or books or wife:
When Vellum thus, in flatt'ring strain,
Did certain gainful views maintain.
"—Genius like yours, profound, refin'd,
Inspiring such an active mind,
Cannot sit still beneath the shade
Which your name has immortal made,
But must in those pursuits engage
Which both improve and charm the age,
And I my services commend
To my learn'd patron and my friend;
From whom I've had a letter'd store,
And only want a little more."
"'Tis very true," replied the Sage,
" That I have many a scatter'd page,
Which I may still collect together,
In wint'ry nights and rainy weather:
But as I think again in town
My time-worn phiz will not be shown,

You for your own, or for my sake,
Or both perhaps, a tour must make,
And fetch the Learning from the Lake."
—Thus with kind words from head and heart,
These friendly folk were seen to part:
Vellum's rich hopes were running o'er,
And Syntax gain'd an added store
To what from Sommerden he brought,
When he, with nuptial fancies fraught,
The promis'd smiles of Hymen sought.
—As he pass'd on, St. Paul's hoarse bell
Struck, as he said, the welcome knell
Of his departure, to regain
The blessings of his Sylvan reign,
Impress'd with this delightful thought,
A calm but short night's rest he sought.

CANTO XXXVIII

THE morning smil'd, and ere the clock
    Had the mark'd hour of seven struck,
The breakfast, plac'd in order due,
Presented plenty to their view,
For Mrs. Broom had taken care
What the time could allow was there;
And, on the journey, should they feel
To munch a jig-jog trav'lling meal,
A sausage, big as one-pound rocket,
Had found its way to Patrick's pocket,
With such assistances as might
Give relish to the passing bite.
The nurse and foundling too were there,
To hear a blessing and a prayer
For those propitious smiles of Heaven
Which oft to pious hopes are given.
What pass'd besides, I need not tell,
The words were kind, and meant farewell.

The Doctor now bestrode his mare,
And calmly mov'd across the Square,
But soon more gaily trotted on,
And as he pass'd through Highgate town,
In pensive gaze he wander'd o'er
A scene he should behold no more,
And felt inspired to invoke
St. Paul's high dome, but, ere he spoke,
Its noble form was lost in smoke:

Nor did his Muse or mind agree
To praise what he no more could see.
Besides, the creature he bestrode
Was not for thinking on the road;
She was of an high-mettled breed,
An eager-pacing, lively steed,
Active, but a well-temper'd creature,
Sprightly her name, as was her nature;
Not as old *Grizzle* e'er had been,
And as poor *Punch* was lately seen,
To sober paces early taught,
On whom the rider's serious thought
Might be indulg'd, from trotting free,
In silence or soliloquy.
It seem'd her wish, as was her power,
To trot eight miles within the hour.
Without a touch of whip or spur
To set her motions on the stir:
Nay, 'twas alone the tighten'd rein
That could her quick'ning steps restrain.

The earlier hours of morn were past,
When speed repress'd, there came at last,
To suit the Sage, the tranquil hour
When thought could re-assume its power,
And the calm spirit of his breast
Thus weigh'd the feelings it possess'd:
" In this same matrimonial dance
It seems I stand but little chance:
As for the widows I have seen,
They rather serv'd my mind to wean
From cheering hopes of those delights
Which ought to flow from marriage rites.
Whoe'er those curious dames may find
In matrimonial bonds to bind,

If charms in them they chance to see,
Must have far diff'rent tastes from me.
In London I soon found 'twas vain
For me to try a bride to gain:
Alas, how I was there beguil'd!
I gain'd no *wife*, but found a *child*.
The Darling Pallet might have prov'd
An object worthy to be lov'd:
But soon the fair-one made it known
That her warm heart was not her own;
Nor could I hope, had it been free,
She would bestow that heart on me.
With charms she does from nature claim,
And fortune waiting upon fame,
To favour I could ne'er pretend
But as a fond, admiring friend.—
Such then has been my outward tour;
Nor can I hope from fortune's store,
My journey home will give me more.
—In such a semi-grumbling tone
He mutter'd as he travell'd on;
When, to his unexpecting eyes,
High spiry tow'rs appear'd to rise,
That crown'd a noble mansion's state
Whose ancient figure mark'd the date
Of grandeur, which worth could attain
In our Eliza's glorious reign.
He view'd the woods that spread around
The wide extent of various ground,
The verdant lawns, th' embosom'd glades
Which court the branchy, sylvan shades;
The crystal stream that winds between,
And, where it flows, reflects the scene,
Enliven'd by the dappled breed,
Whose ranging herd unnumber'd feed.

IN SEARCH OF A WIFE

Scarce need I say his eye pursued,
With warm delight, the place he view'd.
—Now Syntax, though in humble state,
Bent him not low to rich or great,
Unless their virtues did supply
Life's more commanding dignity.
He felt the honour that was due
To station, and he paid it too;
But would scarce yield a flatt'ring word
To one who was a mere MY LORD.
He knew that wealth well understood
Has ample powers of doing good.
He therefore bent the willing knee,
Where it flowed forth in charity;
But he could the rich man disdain
Whose coffers overflow'd in vain;
And titled greatness he defied
Which dealt forth scorn and cherish'd pride.
Hence he, in calm parsonic state,
Approach'd the lordly mansion gate,
With neither more nor less of fame
Than he was conscious he could claim,
Due to a pious pastor's name.
There, 'neath a grand antique arcade,
For coolness or reflection made,
He saw Sir John, on thought intent,
Who 'gainst a Gothic column leant:
The Lord of this so princely place
Was walking by with solemn grace;
For on his breast was seen from far
The glitt'ring of his silver star.
This Syntax saw through branches green,
Before that he himself was seen:
But soon as his known form appear'd
The Knight aloud the Doctor cheer'd,

Nor was my Lord a whit behind
In words that mark'd a welcome kind,
And promise of the friendly care
That waited his reception there.
"Doctor," he said, "you now are come,
To where, I tell you, 'be at home':
And if you wish your host to please,
O let him see you quite at ease!
Nay, I will take it more than kind,
If by no needless form confin'd,
You will pursue your willing pleasure
According to your fancied measure.
The life we lead here, you will see,
Is not without variety:
Consult your fancy then and chuse
Whate'er around will best amuse.
Such is the wish that I make known,
And now I leave you to Sir John;
Who will to all your thoughts attend,
As your good *Cicerone* friend."
—All this kind ceremony done,
Syntax was to his chamber shown,
Where Patrick waited to prepare
The toilette with attentive care,
For much he wish'd his skill to show,
In turning Syntax to a beau.
"I must," he said, "try all my art,
To make your Rev'rence very smart:
A valet's skill I long since knew
In the gay camp and quarters too;
For here are ladies I have seen
Each of them fine as any queen,
And therefore, Sir, you must be dress'd
To-day, at least, in all your best."—
"Then be it so," the Sage replied,
"Yours is an honest proper pride,

Nor do I now, good Pat, conceal
How I approve your active zeal:
So turn all out, and let me see
My better show of drapery."
—This done, Pat labour'd to unfurl
The wig into a dropping curl,
That done, and nicely powder'd o'er,
It was a grizzle wig no more.
—The neat, new pumps, in London made,
By a fam'd artist in his trade,
And the silk hose then took their turn,
Which feet and legs had never worn;
With a canonic suit of black,
That had but twice adorn'd his back.
His long chin Syntax self had shear'd
Of a stiff three days' grisly beard;
Then scrubb'd with soap, whose fine perfume
Distill'd a fragrance through the room.
Pat to his neckcloth gave an air
In style and à la militaire:
His pocket too a 'kerchief bore
With scented water sprinkled o'er.
Thus bang'd up, sweeten'd and clean-shav'd,
The Sage the dinner-table brav'd:
Between two beauties he was seated,
And with such kind attention greeted,
That he could not have hop'd for more,
Had he rich Durham's mitre bore.
As he drew in his chair he bow'd,
When, looking on each side he vow'd,
He felt himself a coat of arms,
Supported by angelic charms.
Thus with fine sentiments he warm'd;
With his gay, brilliant sallies charm'd,
And, by his Quixote tales, gave birth
From time to time, to such keen mirth

That the high Lady of the feast
Declar'd he in himself possess'd
The leading powers that impart
Perfection to dramatic art;
That his bold, lofty thoughts rehearse
The tragic dignity of verse;
That in his sketches after nature
There's Comedy in ev'ry feature,
And in his stories Farce appears,
Broad laugh to wake almost to tears.
Nor did my Lady think alone;
The thought was that of ev'ry one.

Three days were past, and not a void
Was known in pleasure unemploy'd:
Luxurious plenty crown'd the board,
And reason was the sov'reign lord
That did the splendid scene controul;—
Whether it were the flow of soul,
Or fancy's sport, or active play,
Time pass'd delightfully away,
And Syntax was rejoic'd to see
He added to the gaiety.
—Among the rest, the jovial chace
Was a known pleasure of the place,
And he by his kind Lady friend
Was warmly summoned to attend
As her Equerry in the field:
To her commands most proud to yield,
He there appear'd, in sprightly glee,
Be-capp'd in due conformity;
For, to give him a sportsman's air,
Some fair hand did his cap prepare.
He canter'd by my Lady's side
Who undertook to be his guide;

A NOBLE HUNTING PARTY

IN SEARCH OF A WIFE

But when the hounds had caught the scent
Swift as the wind my Lady went:
She was the Dian of the day,
O'er hill and dale she brush'd away,
And left the Doctor to pursue
The pack, which never caught his view.
But whether that he could not keep
His saddle as he took a leap,
Or by what strange mischance he fell,
He could not, or he would not tell:
Between two banks he was seen sprawling,
And loud enough for mercy calling.
He found himself 'midst prickly bushes,
Half smother'd with dead leaves and rushes;
While sportsmen, as he shudder'd there,
Pass'd all above him through the air;
Like an old broomstick-mounted witch,
They each flew o'er him in the ditch,
Exclaiming, "Sir, lie snug and warm,
And you'll not come to any harm!"
But when he thought they all were over,
He scrambled mainly from his cover.
His rambling horse was quickly caught,
When he the welcome mansion sought,
Bespatter'd o'er with mud and dirt,
But sound in limb and quite unhurt;
And in the luncheon's morning ration
He sought and found his recreation.

My Lady had the story heard,
And when at dinner she appear'd,
Enquired as if she nothing knew
How he had kept from out her view,
And what he with himself had done
Throughout the morning's glorious run

He told his tale, 'twas such a treat,
That they could scarcely drink or eat,
It produc'd such food for laughter
Both during dinner and long after,
"When you put on your wings and flew,
And vanish'd quickly from my view,
Forc'd to my fortune to submit,
I fell," he said, "into a pit;
And such appear'd my wretched birth,
I thought that I had run to earth,
And should require no other aid
Than an old sexton and a spade."
"Well," said my Lord, "no sport shall break
Or even risk the Doctor's neck,
For the next hunting morning, he
Shall pass his better hours with me
In hunting through my library."
"Alas, my Lord," the Doctor said,
"I wish that you could be obey'd,
But I must add that, to my sorrow,
My sporting here will end to-morrow:
For I have other game in view,
Another chace I must pursue:
I, my good Lord, must cease to roam,
And turn my willing steps tow'rds home.
I there have friends to whom I owe
The ev'ry comfort which I know,
And they a kind impatience show
To see their Pastor once again
Among his flock at Sommerden."
"—I'm sorry, if it must be so,"
A soft voice said, "but ere you go,
Try to persuade your friend Sir John
To take a wife, nor live alone.
He has great wealth and ancient birth,
And is possess'd of real worth,

Yet so wrong-headed he prefers
To swell the list of bachelors.
I tell you, Doctor, what is true,
And now I leave him, Sir, to you."
Syntax replied—" I will obey—
And now, Sir Knight, mind what I say.
I'm but an organ rather rude
Of one most excellently good,
Though, as I speak by her decree,
I claim all due authority.
—I have been married and can state
The pleasures that on marriage wait;
I know what 'tis to lose a wife,
The pride and comfort of my life;
Nor does a day pass o'er my head,
But I lament my Dolly dead:
Then listen as your Syntax preaches
The doctrine his experience teaches.
Of wisest maxims this is one,
It is not good to live alone:
'Tis grievous through life's path to stray
Without companions on the way;
If it were only thus to say:
How very glorious is the sight,
Now the sun, in its utmost height,
Tinges with gold the wood-clad hill,
While its beams glisten on the rill!
—With what a grace that myrtle grows!
How fragrant is that op'ning rose!
How sweet the bird that does prolong
The vernal ev'ning with a song!
But O what joy their hearts will prove,
Who, as they journey, say, *We love!*
—When ills the married pair betide,
Each feels a comfort or a guide:

For we will not exceptions make
Which captious minds may chuse to take:
And if a marriage proves a pain,
If it should feel a galling chain,
It is the fault of those who bear it;
They forge it first before they wear it:
They merit all that they endure
Who feel the evils they could cure.
When ills assail, who has not seen
That sufferings have lessen'd been,
When they participation prove
From friendship, tenderness or love?
How soon the fretful pain grows less,
When kind hearts share in the distress:
Nay sorrow almost disappears,
When each wipes off the other's tears:
'Tis better, though it still annoys,
Than many things the world calls joys.
The wifeless man retains his pleasure
But a short time, whate'er its measure;
And his vexations all grow stronger,
Nay, which is worse, they last the longer:
While he who has a tender heart
In a wife's breast, and will impart
All that he feels within his own,
The cheering thought, the sigh, the moan,
Will two-fold ev'ry pleasure know
And take but half his share of woe."
—Sir John replied with gentle grace,
But smile sarcastic on his face:
"All this is very fine you say
About life's matrimonial way,
Where, though sometimes a flow'ret blows,
Yet there are prickles on the rose;
And may we not have cause to mourn,
When we are wounded by a thorn?

But then, besides these self-same thorns,
Hymen is sometimes crown'd with horns."
"—Whose fault is that?" Syntax replied,
"Treat your wife always as a bride,
And let your honeymoon survive,
'Till one or other cease to live.
Be good, be kind, love as you ought,
The wife will rarely be in fault:
'Tis want of husband's love and care
That plants those ugly branches there.
O cultivate the nuptial soil
With fond affection's anxious toil;
Where, if love's fragrant flowers you sow,
Nor Thorns nor Horns will ever grow.
And now, my worthy friend, Sir John,
My grave, appointed task is done."—
He ceas'd and bow'd, when, all around,
Praise did in ev'ry form abound:
The ladies scream'd out with applause
For pleading thus the female cause:
While one from off her finger took
A ring, and with a gracious look
Bade him the brilliant trifle take
And wear it for her sex's sake:
While Sir John said, "my shame to smother,
Accept, I pray you, such another.
Impute it to my stupid brain
That thus you preach, and preach in vain.
The time may come when Cupid's arrow
May set in flow my frozen marrow;
Or when bright eyes their beams may dart,
And wake my now too slumb'ring heart:
Then, when to marry is my lot,
I'll send to you to tie the knot."
—Thus the enliven'd ev'ning pass'd
And all were sorry 'twas the last;

For not alone the Doctor's sense,
His scholarship and eloquence
Had given the hours a quicker flow
Than common conversations do;
But he possess'd the power to please
By his mild eccentricities.
—The parting words were very kind,
Nor in the common form design'd,
Just to be civil and no more,
To be forgot the following hour;
But such as were to virtue due,
And were the boon of friendship too.

The following morn and when the sun
Had scarce three hours his course begun,
Syntax was trotting on his way,
And a long journey clos'd the day:
Nor was it 'till the third day's end
That he shook hands with Dickey Bend.
—Here he well knew he could impart
The secret wishes of his heart;
Here tell his late adventures o'er
And all his future hopes explore,
While friendship would its aid prepare
To grant the wish or soothe the care.
Nor did he for a day postpone
To make his hopes and wishes known.—
The provost answer'd:—"My dear friend,
You know full well you may depend
On all that I can say or do
To forward the important view,
That I may venture to presage
Does your whole anxious mind engage.
You wish another wife to gain,
Nor will the wish be made in vain,

If, as I hope, you will approve
The lady offer'd to your love.
Of my dear wife a friend most dear
To-morrow is expected here;
Who, if I do not greatly err,
In manners, form, and character
Is just the fair you would prefer.
You will not startle, if 'tis said
She may be call'd an ancient maid,
But then, to give the maid her due,
My friend, she's young enough for you,
Of my wife's age, and to be free,
My wife is young enough for me.
If the Divine and learned Sage
Wishes a plaything for his age,
She's still so fashion'd as to prove
What reason can demand of love.
She has enough of what is good
To fill your void of widowhood;
A lady bred, and, I can tell,
She tickles the piano well:
And truly, speaking of the heart,
Her bosom bears your counterpart.
There's fortune too, a pretty thing,
T' enrich the matrimonial ring.
Her nuptial prospects have miscarried,
But still she wishes to be married;
And my wife says it is her aim
To bear a known and learned name:
A fact, I think, the truth secures,
When I declare that name is yours."
Syntax exclaim'd, "Aye, this would do!
'Tis a fair prospect to the view,
But my stars must be rul'd by you."
—The following day the lady came:
Nor need I tell her maiden name,

For ere a week or so was o'er
That maiden name was hers no more.
On the third day kind Mrs. Bend,
Who with both, as a mutual friend,
Had talk'd the important matter over,
Presented Syntax as a lover;
While Dickey whisper'd, "push it well,
And you'll soon bear away the belle;
Let her know all that you can do;
And Miss, fear not, will buckle to."—
The lady, as for many a year
Soft things were strangers to her ear,
Seem'd to be carried by surprise,
For high-flown thoughts and gentle sighs
Possess'd, it seems, the wish'd-for power,
And she said AYE within the hour,
Nay, on the third or fourth day after,
They were both noos'd in Hymen's garter.
—Nought now was heard but *Love* and *Dear*,
My Dear go there! *my Love* come here!
And, since it is such charming weather,
O let us take a stroll together!
While she would sing to some fine tune,
"Our life shall be one honeymoon."
Thus it appear'd, and Dickey Bend
Rejoic'd to see his happy friend;
And only wish'd the joy might last
When many a future year was past.
—Patrick to Sommerden was sent
To tell the tale of this event,
And to employ his utmost care
How to receive the nuptial pair.
He with great glee the tidings carried:
And that his Reverence was married

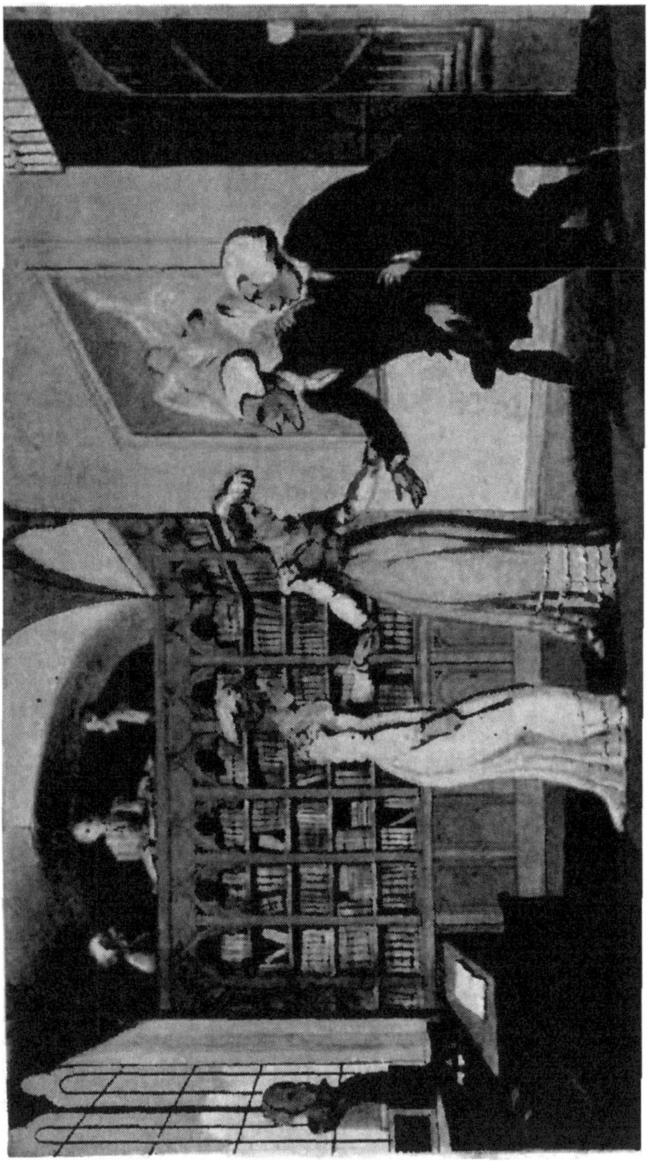

Did ev'ry village tongue employ
To tell its wonder and its joy.
The WORTHIES were but lately come
Back to their long deserted home,
And felt it as a sad disaster
To be without their much-lov'd pastor:
But still it touch'd a doubtful string
The kind of wife that he would bring.—
Syntax to his friends had written,
"That he had been by reason smitten;
That he was not so very stupid
As to play a game with Cupid;
But he had found a proper wife
Who, he believ'd, would through his life
Strive to exert her various powers
In quickening his slow-pacing hours,
And that 'twould be her constant aim
To be an honour to his name:
She, he was sure, would gain her ends,
To charm himself and please his friends."—
Pat, who had seen both great and small,
Was ask'd, and he confirm'd it all.
"A lady of genteeler air,"
He said, "was not seen anywhere;
Nor is there one about the Lake
Who will a better figure make:
On Thursday next they will be here,
And the whole parish will appear
In its best figure and array,
To celebrate the holiday,
When my dear master comes again
With his fine Bride to Sommerden."

The day arriv'd, the sun shone bright,
And ev'ry face gay with delight,

The motley crowd were seen to wait
Impatient at the village gate;
And when the expected pair appear'd,
One gen'ral voice of joy was heard.
The Bride, whose tonish inclination
Attended to the ruling fashion,
To make her entry had bedress'd
Her upright form in all her best,
And thought it a becoming care
To make the natives gaze and stare.
The plumage nodded from her head,
Her pale cheeks wore a tint of red;
And, as the carriage pass'd along,
She bow'd to the admiring throng:
Nay, scatter'd silver 'mong the boys
Whose huzzas join'd the jovial noise.
Some lin'd the paths beside the road,
And some the way with branches strew'd.
Four damsels of superior grace,
The humble beauties of the place,
By *Worthy's* care all clad in white,
With rose-red ribbons gay bedight,
A garland bore, whose flow'rs combine
To make the nuptial symbol fine;
And Sal and Kate and Doll and Betty
Were never known to look so pretty;
While many a tender village swain
View'd them and own'd a lover's pain.
The steeple bells were loudly ringing,
The parish choir preceded singing,
Accompanied by fifes and drums,
"Behold the conq'ring hero comes."
Ma'am own'd she felt no small delight
At this unlook'd-for rural sight,
But felt it more because it prov'd
How much the Doctor was belov'd.

IN SEARCH OF A WIFE

—The long procession mov'd on strait
To the old hall's wide op'ning gate,
Where *Worthy* and his charming mate
Stood with kind smiles upon their faces,
And their known hospitable graces,
The married couple to receive
With the best welcome they could give.—
" The husband," Syntax said, " commends
His dear wife to his best of friends."—
" The love we to that husband bear
That dear wife will most fondly share."
The 'Squire replied; when to her breast
Madam receiv'd the bridal guest.
—The bride at once felt she was come
To where she found an instant home:
Such cheerful kindness did appear,
The wish to please look'd so sincere,
The forms which well-bred manners boast
Were in frank ease so quickly lost,
That ere an hour or two were o'er
The stranger feel was felt no more;
And Mrs. Syntax gladly found,
Ere she could throw her thoughts around,
A husband kind, by all belov'd,
And friends her heart at once approv'd.
—The crowd retreated to the green,
Where a sheep roasting whole was seen;
And many a stream of ale encreas'd
The pleasure of the joyous feast;
While song and dance and pastimes gay
Conclude the Hymeneal day.

Thus hope on future prospects smil'd,
Nor was it of its views beguil'd.
The higher class of neighbours came
To visit the new-married dame,

And all delighted were to see
The Mistress of the Rectory:
Nay, the gay Ladies round the Lake
Did from her dress the fashion take.
At first, she seem'd but stiff and starch,
And walk'd as upright as a larch,
But she knew when to condescend
And to the due occasion bend.
She saw that former modes of life
Would suit not with a Parson's wife;
She therefore pass'd the farmer's gate
And chatted with his flatter'd mate;
Would ask a chair and sit before
The threshold of the cottage door;
Call forth the children from within,
And stroke the head and chuck the chin,
Praise the attentive parents' care,
And talk of favours they should share,
If she the active fruits should see
Of virtue and of industry.
Though in her bounties unrestrain'd,
She still her dignity maintain'd;
Though she would at the cottage call,
And talk in gentle speech to all;
Yet when she thus impos'd her law,
Their love was not unmix'd with awe.
Thus she assum'd the village reign,
Nor did she bear the rule in vain;
And oft-times both the WORTHIES bless'd
The new-brought treasure they possess'd.
—Thus, while she gave the village place
Another and a better face,
Syntax a change had undergone,
By which at first he scarce was known.
—He now a varying semblance wore
From what he ever seem'd before.

He now a diff'rent form was seen, ⎫
So nicely dress'd and always clean, ⎬
He might be taken for a Dean: ⎭
Besides, as Pat was heard to say,
His chin was clean-shav'd ev'ry day.
Nay, while in contemplative mood,
His various studies he pursued,
Not as it us'd to be before,
In some old coat to threadbare wore:
He now in robe of purple dye,
Maintain'd Canonic dignity.
His gaiters with dust cover'd o'er
Were seen upon his legs no more,
But when he rode, the top-boots shone,
Or hussar'd *à la Wellington*.
The squeez'd-up hat that deck'd his brow
Was chang'd to solemn beaver now:
His queer, grey caxon laid aside,
A smart brown wig the place supplied,
Which, manag'd well with comb and care,
The semblance bore of native hair.
Thus chang'd, the wond'ring people star'd,
And the first time that he appear'd
At church in all this novel gear,
There scarce was one attentive ear;
The gaping wonder and surprise
Forc'd all the soul into the eyes.
—The gentry much admir'd the art
That made the learned sloven smart;
And all around approv'd the dame
Who quietly contriv'd the same:
But she had something more to do,
To change his gen'ral manners too.
—His violin was not unstrung,
But only touch'd when Madam sung;
Or when the Lady chose by chance
To join the *Worthies* in a dance:

No more he fiddled to the people,
When they bejigg'd it 'neath the steeple;
No more he prais'd the most adroit,
Who urg'd the ball or threw the quoit;
But still the people all around him
As kind and friendly ever found him,
As when he wore a six-days' beard
And in his grizzle wig appear'd.
He still smil'd 'mong the village folk,
Though he left off his funny joke;
And such was the continual good
Which they in word or deed pursued,
That when he and his stately Lady
Stroll'd round the village, 'twas a gay day.

The winter came, the winds were bleak,
And the cold breeze blew o'er the Lake,
When Madam Syntax never stirr'd
But well beruff'd and well befurr'd.
While the Sage was to public view
Wrapp'd-up and well bemuffled too.
His neck was bound with hairy skin,
That form'd a pillow for his chin:
So careful did the Dame appear,
To guard from cold her swaddled dear.
—Some hinted, 'twas a silly whim,
To deck the Doctor in this trim,
And make him look so like a bear
Whose skin he thus was seen to wear;
But that these fancies prov'd of course
The Grey Mare was the better Horse.
How that might be I cannot tell,
But this was known—all things went well,
And if her fancy was for sway,
She rul'd by seeming to obey.
The WORTHIES too, who Syntax lov'd,
The new-born changes much approv'd:

They joy'd to see his alter'd phiz,
That he no longer was a quiz;
And were delighted at the plan
That made him look a Gentleman;
That his exterior might not err
From his pure, native character.

On moonlight nights the neighbours round
Or music or card-parties found,
All in due form and social glee,
Or at the Hall or Rectory;
While each, in some kind welcome way,
Did hospitable rites repay.
The higher show, the Christmas ball,
Were the display of Worthy-Hall;
While lesser pleasures did engage
Th' attentions of the Parsonage:
But, in regard and kindness shown,
These families appear'd as one.
—Thus pleasantly the Winter pass'd,
When ling'ring Spring arriv'd at last;
And when it was now growing gay
With the sweet offerings of May,
A Letter to the Doctor came
Inscrib'd with sweet Miss PALLET's name.

" You know, DEAR SIR, I did intend
To pay a visit to my friend,
As well for his dear, rev'rend sake,
As to steal beauties from the Lake,
And let my pencil ramble round
The charms of that enchanted ground.
But sage discretion bids delay
To future time my northern way:
For I had promis'd that my care
To Keswick's side the child should bear;

But if with nurse and child I travel,
A score of tongues would soon unravel,
By scandal tutor'd, the strange sight
Of poor Miss Pallet's distant flight;
And all the spiteful world would join
To swear the little Bantling's mine.
I think you will with this agree,
And praise my cautious prudery,
If I defer my course to steer
To Keswick 'till another year.
The Boy's a perfect Cherub grown,
And the good nurse will bring him down;
I trust within a day or two
She will her northern tour pursue,
And soon present the babe to you.
But though his is a wayward fate,
I cannot but congratulate
The little urchin, since he shares
In your kind heart a parent's cares:
And be assur'd, my Dear Divine,
That he has gain'd a share in mine.
My best respects I pray make known
To one whom now you call your own;
And when to Heaven you urge your prayer,
O ask its all-protecting care
For one, who does her name commend
To the remembrance of her friend!
That name, as you've been us'd to call it,
Is your most grateful,   S<small>ARAH</small> P<small>ALLET</small>."

In a few days the bantling came,
Whom now we *Little Johnny* name,
And Mrs. Syntax thought the story
So added to the Doctor's glory,
That she seem'd proud of *Little John*,
As if the babe had been her own.

Though sprinkled from the sacred rill
Of parish-church on Holborn-Hill,
She would it were baptis'd again
With all due form at Sommerden;
And so it was, when *Worthy's* self
Stood sponsor for the little elf;
And Madam Syntax held it there
With promise of her future care.
Each ceremonial rite was done,
Again the child was christen'd John:
No other name, alas was known.
To give the name it ought to bear,
No parents did the duty share,
Th' unnat'ral parents were not there,
But such as happy chance had sent,
Or Heaven had in its mercy lent.
—The Register, as all may see,
Records th' eventful history.

All things pass'd on in that calm way
Which leaves description nought to say.
—All that the Doctor found of leisure
From parish cares and social pleasure
Was to his Study's toil confin'd;
Where ev'ry impulse of his mind
Was urg'd to gratify the aim,
On basis firm to fix his claim
To Learning's meed and future Fame:
And when Ma'am's busy morn was o'er
Among her birds, her flowers and poor,
She was beheld in silent pride
Embroid'ring at his table's side:
Nay, oft-times she would fetch the book
In which enquiry ask'd to look,
And having found the wish'd-for page,
Would smile and say: " Look there, my Sage ! "

—Thus hours and days and seasons went
As it appear'd in full content:
At least complaint in silence slept,
Or was a perfect secret kept.
During the summer *Dickey Bend*
With Madam visited his friend,
And joy'd to find their nuptial scheme
Had not turn'd out an idle dream,
Fair *Pallet* also came to glean
The charms of the surrounding scene,
And gladly bore away to town
The beauties she had made her own.
Nay, *Vellum* also did repair
To talk of print and paper there;
And, in due time, he bore away
The treasure of a future day,
Which the learn'd Author had prepar'd
With promise of no slight reward.

At length another year pass'd o'er
Just as the last had done before:
Syntax ne'er utter'd a complaint,
And Madam was a perfect saint.
The gout indeed gave hints, though slight,
Just to disturb his sleepy night,
And certain feels to her would say,
Upon a cold and shiv'ring day,
You're not so young, fair dame, we trow,
As you were twenty years ago:
But then, all these complaints to smother,
They were such nurses to each other!
The foundling also 'gan to walk,
And which was better still, to talk:
Nay, Mrs. Syntax oft would quote
His sayings in imperfect note;

Was pleas'd when he could say, "*Your Tab!*"
But more so when he said "*Mamma!*"
A fondling sound that did appear
So pleasing to her ready ear.

Just at this time the evening fair,
With a soft breeze of summer air,
Dear Mrs. S—— propos'd to take
A little fishing on the Lake.
Pat did the usual boat prepare,
The lines and angle-rods were there,
When the sage Doctor plied the oar,
And cautious row'd along the shore.
Madam stood upright in the boat,
And eager ey'd the bobbing float;
When, by what shock no one could tell,
Into the flood the Lady fell:
Instant he plung'd into the wave,
The darling of his life to save,
When *Patrick* follow'd, nothing loth,
And flound'ring, nearly drown'd them both:
But they were near the grassy shore,
And all the danger soon was o'er.
The wet clothes chang'd from foot to head,
The fright dispell'd, and both in bed,
They somehow had the secret charm
To hug and keep each other warm.
The *Worthies* hurried down to see
The mischief at the Rectory;
But, finding ev'ry thing was right,
And Ma'am recover'd from her fright,
To keep alarming thoughts away,
They ask'd for some amusing play,
And soon the welcome cards were spread
On either corner of the bed.

The curious scene throughout gave birth
To bursts of unexpected mirth,
'Till the kind friends, the visit over,
Left them to sleep and to recover.

    The following morn, as they talk'd o'er
The dangers of the day before,
Syntax began to shake and shiver,
While ev'ry limb was seen to quiver:
He wish'd to treat his state with laughter:—
" O hissing hot into the water
I popp'd, 'tis true, as I may say
With old Jack Falstaff in the play;
And as it harm'd not him, d'ye see,
I think it cannot injure me;
Such flesh had he to work upon,
And I am nought but skin and bone."
Poor Mrs. S—— big with alarms,
And all her fears and frights in arms,
Could not help saying:—"'Tis provoking!
At such a time you should be joking!"
When he with chatt'ring teeth replied,
" My love lay all your fears aside:
And as I do not feel alarm,
When I'm so cold, be not so warm!"
Though he, indeed, as it appears,
Let loose his jokes to calm her fears.—
—But not a moment was delay'd,
To send for neighb'ring Doctor's aid.
The Doctor in a hurry came,
And found the system in a flame:
—The lancet to profusion bled,
The blisters cover'd back and head
And Syntax was convey'd to bed.
When there reclin'd, his upward eye
Seem'd as commercing with the sky,

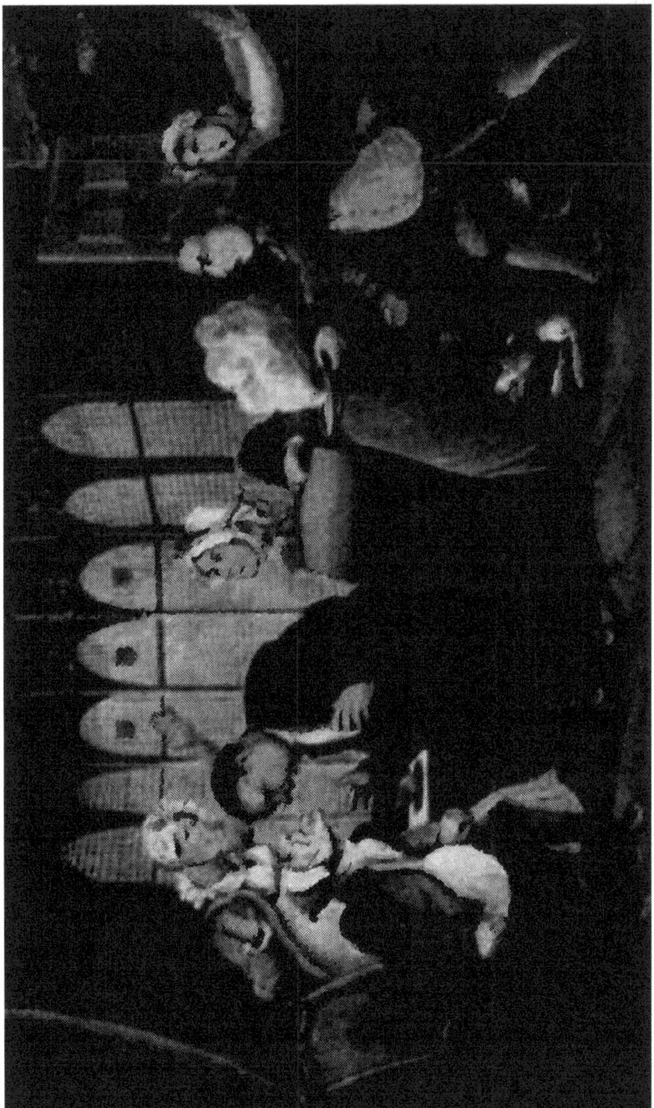

And his hand wav'd, as if to tell,
This is a long and last farewell!
Torpor then o'er his senses crept,
And he appear'd as if he slept;
But Death had given the final stroke,
For from that sleep he ne'er awoke:
Nor will he e'er again awake,
Until Creation's self shall shake,
And the last Trump its silence break,
To call him, with a life renew'd,
To the bright guerdon of the Good.

When the good man had breath'd his last,
Poor Mrs. Syntax stood aghast,
Then laid her pale cheek to his face,
And clasp'd him in a long embrace:
Nor did she on the horror wait
To contemplate the work of fate;
But to the *Hall* in hurry hied,
With little *Johnny* by her side.
She told her state, pale as despair,
And fill'd the house with sorrow there.
—Thus SYNTAX clos'd his life's career,
With all to hope and nought to fear.—
The frequent tear still in his eyes,
Worthy prepar'd the obsequies,
With all due rites to grace the end
Of his belov'd, lamented friend.
O 'twas a melancholy scene
When he was borne along the green!
What train of mourners did appear,
And scarce an eye without a tear!
No toil the harvest fields display,
It seem'd grief's mournful holiday.
The village wept—the hamlets round
Crowded the consecrated ground;

And waited there to see the end
Of Pastor, Teacher, Father, Friend!
—When in the cold ground he was laid,
Poor Patrick from his trembling spade
Could scarce the light dust scatter o'er
The form which he should see no more.—
—At first the bursting sorrow came
In floods upon the widow'd Dame,
But, by affection's care consol'd,
Unruly grief was soon controul'd:
Religion too had taught her mind
Its law divine, to be resign'd:
Though, for the rankling, heart-felt wound,
A perfect cure was never found.
O 'twas a loss!—The Blessing flew;
Th' enjoyment and the prospect too!
It was a tranquil, calm delight;
No glare—but ev'ry day was bright!
—Through life's lone way she travell'd on,
In gloomy guise, with *Little John*.
The relict of the man they lov'd,
She still the *Worthies'* kindness prov'd;
While *Dickey Bend* and his fond wife
Had been and were her friends through life.-
—But, once a year, affection's claim
The Pilgrim Widow always came,
To Sommerden, to shed a tear
Beside his tomb who died for her:
And *Little John*, as there he knelt,
Was taught to weep for what she felt!
And, as he wept he scarce knew why,
Lisp'd the instinctive agony.

The TOMB near path-way side appear'd,
' By *Worthy's* sadden'd friendship rear'd:

The FUNERAL of SYNTAX.

Near it the dark, o'erspreading yew
Sheds tears of morn and evening dew;
And, as the sculpture meets the eye,
"ALAS, POOR SYNTAX!" with a sigh,
Is read by every passer-by:
And wakes the pensive thought, sincere,
For ever sad!—for ever dear!——

My verse has now no more to tell.——
The Story's done.—*SYNTAX FAREWELL!*

FINIS.

Lightning Source UK Ltd.
Milton Keynes UK
UKHW020735140922
408851UK00005B/533